CABRIOLETS

JEAN~PAUL THEVENET
PETER VANN

CABRIOLETS

Preface by Gérald Asaria

Motorbooks International
Publishers & Wholesalers Inc
Osceola, Wisconsin 54020, USA ®

ACKNOWLEDGEMENTS

The authors would like to thank all those who helped shoulder the burden of work with such good spirits. In particular they wish to thank the following:

Rodney and Annie Abensur, AGM,
Automobiles Citroën, L'Aventure Peugeot,
Lucien-François Bernard, BMW A.G., Peter Briggs,
Jean-Jacques Cribier, Thierry Culliford,
Jean-Pierre Delaunay, Raymond Dierickx,
Sté Embraer, Ivan Ginioux, Johnny Hassan,
John H. Haynes, Jérôme Heyndrickx,
Charles Howard, Daniel Isaac, Denys Joannon,
André Lecoq, Guy Martinez,
Dudley Mason-Styrron, Francesco Mirabile,
Musée de l'Automobiliste, Musée de Vendée,
Marc Nicolosi, Jean-Antoine Personnaz, Porsche A.G.,
Charles Pozzi-Ferrari, Mario Righini,
Rolls-Royce Motors International,
F. P. Tsaropoulos, Unijet - Leadair,
Patrick Van der Stricht, Hélène Wittmer.

J.-P. Thévenet
Peter Vann

PREFACE

There are certain things in life which one would love to achieve. Even before coming across the first draft of this album, I knew that this would be one of those things. All I needed was to see the glimmering metal body of the Rolls–Royce Springfield, the aggressiveness of the Delahaye 135 or the sparkling colours of the Thunderbird 59 to inspire me to put pen to paper, to give the information that the picture could not convey by itself: the legends and myths that emanate from the photographs, the statistics or the technical references which the eye cannot see.

To put down on paper, however glossy it is, the spirit of an admirable three-dimensional form needs considerable talent. Peter Vann's pictures have the necessary balance of strength, colour and harmony which can make any car stand out. He was attracted by the purity of the form of these prestige cars, as other people are impressed by the power of the Formula 1. Peter Vann has the ability to bestow nobility onto a Traction 11B. What was asked of Peter Vann was to add a dream-like quality to the reality of the subject.

I find nothing more tedious than reading the curriculum vitaes of an author in a preface (even if they have been prettified by a writer's pen or the McIntosh PC of a friend recruited for the occasion). I am therefore going to attempt to give Peter Vann's CV in a few lines. After finishing at the Zurich school of photography, and graduating there, he went on to the stage. He was in the theatre business, and did some singing. At 28 he became an idol of the young thanks to a hit. Several winters later the summer hits were becoming rare in Zurich and he went back to his profession as a photographer, commenting on this change: "It's hard for an idol to become an ant." After several years, this ant made a name for himself as an automobile photographer in France, Germany and Switzerland. Arnauld de Fouchier and EPA Editions (the French publishers) gave him the opportunity in 1983 to express his potential as an artist beyond his needs as a journalist or advertiser with his first album *Automobiles Extraordinaires*. He

crossed the world to capture images of amazing machines and astonished Arnauld and myself when he signed to do this book with me.

Peter, however, with a simplicity which is either due to incredible modesty or to an unknown Swiss sense of humour immediately added: "The most extraordinary thing about this book is not the beauty of the cars nor my photographs but the readers. I still find it hard to believe that there are around 50 000 fans around the world." This fact in this kind of work can be considered a great success, a best-seller which pleases the editor and co-author. That made us think of the birth of a second child: the Cabriolets. Their return to fashion seems unavoidable towards the end of the 1980s even though birds of ill-omen had sent them into oblivion together with luxury, sophistication, the pleasure of driving and the love of that something different.

For a novel, the best-seller recipe seems simple: a good topic, a good author, a good editor, and good marketing. For this kind of album the whole exploit is much more complex. Once the topic and author are identified, the hardest thing still remains to be done: invest an incredible amount of time and effort in the quality of the paper, the quality of the print, trying to make something to measure which will please everyone—and most importantly of all discovering the man who will bring it all together, and give form to this remarkable compilation of pictures. I wrote as much at the beginning of this preface: I would love to have completed this book with Peter Vann, as all the ingredients were there for the mixing. Cars are one of my passions, but not my main activity. Working with Peter Vann required time. Flicking through this book, you are unlikely to realise how many hours of research, how much scouting around, how many miles were covered, and how many risks were involved in the most banal of surroundings. Peter dug up Europe to find these cabriolets, looking out from his car window for days on end to see the shot to make. "Afterwards", he said, "all you have to do is take the photo. It is a cinch even when a coachload of Japanese tourists or a gaggle of geese miraculously appear from nowhere and disturb and liven up a staircase or a parking lot which a moment earlier was deserted".

The person who did this work with Peter Vann is one of the first to have befriended him when he came to Paris. "A real friend." That's how Peter Vann talks of Jean-Paul Thevenet. The rest seems obvious. Thevenet is certainly one of the most accomplished automobile journalists in France. Chief editor, director of the magazine *The Automobile*, he is also a writer, a broadcaster and editor. He has managed to make his passion for four wheels his profession. Even before reading this book I knew that not sharing it with Peter Vann would end up being a pleasure. No person other than Jean-Paul Thevenet could have given these superb pictures that touch of class.

Gérald Asaria

INTRODUCTION

The history of the cabriolet is closely linked to that of the automobile industry. Its own history, though, is wilder, more unpredictable and sometimes even almost crazy. Passion takes a greater place with cabriolets; so much so that the final purpose of this kind of vehicle differs fundamentally from the classic automobile. The standard car has always been carefully thought out and manufactured to get from A to B, in a pleasant manner, but first and foremost came the idea of usefulness. On the other hand, the cabriolet was meant solely for parading about in, to show off the cool character and even arrogance of the privileged people who consider pleasure to be an *art de vivre*.

This may shock those who follow the uncompromising, logical approach to history. What this book aspires to show is that same feeling for the beautiful and useless which caused Gothic spires to be built higher and higher, and which has contributed much more to the automobile industry than repetitive bookish technology. The cabriolet was often conceived to enhance or improve the image of a make of car and it needed to escape from everyday normality, its common sense and desire to satisfy petty requirements. In charge of its design were people who had to create something different, to produce an obvious difference—all before improving on their competitors' designs. It is no surprise that on discovering the cabriolet to be an egotist's car, since it could only take two people, some people immediately went and found a place for a third passenger in a sort of boot right at the back of the body, where these days not even the most docile of domestic animals would deign to travel. Consequently, in the history of a make of car, the appearance of cabriolets is often just a series of ephemeral digressions.

Nor is this book an academic list of models prepared according to convention or reputation. Quite the contrary. Peter Vann and myself took on this work with our reporter's instincts: seeing everything, looking at everything and hearing everything so as to forget nothing. We wanted to remember in the end only what best illustrated the myth, the folly, the supremacy and the magnificence.

In each case Peter photographed first and it was only afterwards, much afterwards, that I related to him the story of his pictures. Acting on reflex, which is often something more important than profound knowledge, his lens managed to capture all its provocativeness, the escapism and even the romantic irony which many a cabriolet stood for. Developing the framework of this book, we kept faith with our first surprised and loving steps towards discovering the automobile: getting to know about something is sharing, is discovering, it means not rushing into things.

We had to define the origins and types of automobiles from which the cabriolet more or less directly derived.

Writing history for historians is dangerously controversial in as much as nothing can be more authentic and authoritative than their own work, so we therefore wisely tried to identify the birth of the cabriolet through the 30 odd makes which represent automobile bodies. In doing this we discovered that, as for most motor vehicles circulating today, the word cabriolet had to be a lasting loan, because the cabriolet was solid and built like a horse carriage.

This horse carriage first made an appearance in the course of the 17th century and was a harnessed vehicle. It had two wheels, two seats and a hood which could be removed if one wanted. The cabriolet's shafts were solidly fixed onto the bodywork. Importantly, the coachman was often the owner of his cabriolet, and therefore right from the start was a man who had no reason to look after his horse or his passenger. With a "giddee-up", the horse gallops off and its movement is passed to the shafts to which it is harnessed. As already mentioned they were an integral part of the bodywork and the unfortunate thing would begin to pitch in time with the sturdy animal. Add to this the fact that in those days road surfaces were always unreliable: going at speed the carriage, which only had one axle, began a frenetic *gigue* which would have caused onlookers to say that it was leaping up and down (the word in French is *cabrioler* which means to caper).

Very soon afterwards, as far as cars were concerned, popular imagination and its common sense identified and called everything that was convertible

7

a "cabriolet". The choice provoked the haughty and controlled fury of master bodybuilders before fashion put the house in order and calmed puritanical historians.

From the outset of the convertible's life, it, not to mention the many others, was reserved for an élite which had to display its social standing. Thus it was essential for the driver to be seen not enjoying the same comfort and protection as the masters in the seats behind who were the sole beneficiaries of the shelter of the hood. The driver drives under the open sky, which is an interesting choice if rain joins in on the outing.

But the snob appeal is far too ostentatious, far too unstylish in its vain provocativeness, with the result that the model soon disappeared to make way for a real interior drive. This incidentally is when the term is first used, as opposed to the preceding model where the driver was literally sitting outside. From then on anything convertible has two or four seats and is called a cabriolet.

These days a clearer but equally indulgent definition allows a cabriolet to be a car with two seats with two side windows and a real boot, not forgetting of course that the rare cabriolets derived from production saloons and at a reasonable price can accommodate four people. This was true, but they wanted to enjoy the open air and the promise of the wind lashing them in the face.

This is why our selection bears for the most part on cabriolets belonging to a period gone forever. Why gone forever? Because the cabriolet was an expensive car to manufacture and expensive to sell. It needed numerous reinforcements and several crossbars to achieve a solid bodywork which could compare with a saloon. What was more, many cabriolets had problems passing the bodywork safety tests, and when it came to fixing the safety belts. Lastly, the hood was a particularly easy prey for thieves and generally for vandals and gave rise to a rare sight today: attacking a work of art or, to put it more simply, a privilege.

Privilege is the word and the aim of this book is to show how it applies to the cabriolet.

Jean-Paul Thevenet

NB: The date next to the precise name of each cabriolet is not when it was launched nor when it first appeared on the market, but rather the year when the model appearing in the photograph was manufactured or first put on the road.

The exact specifications for each car can be found at the end of the book.

CONTENTS

The annual growth in France's automobile production between 1901 and 1907 exceeded 20%. In 1907 France allowed 50 manufacturers to assemble 25,200 cars and to export half. In value these transactions abroad made up 60% of the total exports of the five greats in the automobile industry: France, USA, Great Britain, Germany and Italy. In 1909 over two thousand taxis were driving through the streets of New York, at least a thousand of which were French. Édouard Ballot, who had been manufacturing engines for ships and industrial groups, realised that developing his business meant building car engines, for which there was considerable demand. Thus Delage, Mass and Barré, amongst others, who had been buying De Dion engines gradually procured their supplies from Ballot, giving him a good name at the same time. Then in 1911 he began studying valveless engines with sliding sleeve valves inspired by the Panhard and Levasson techniques. Then the war came along. That and the realisation that the engine was sorted out was good business for the bosses. At the end of the war much had been won and learnt at Ballot. Édouard could now indulge himself in his success as a motorist, but an engine is only ever part of a car. A person who conceives one is a good engineer but the person assembling a car is a great builder and Édouard Ballot was destined to become one of these. His cars even twice won in Indianapolis and achieved international fame.

However, an incredible stroke of bad luck changed all this, but he had already proved his seldom-seen bravery. He then went on to market some magnificent cars, and the three-seater open tourer is a very convincing example of this. Its particularly well-thought out body was made by two master bodybuilders of that time: Lagache and Glasman. Its performance showed it was born in sports competition as it could do more than 110 kph. The curious back window was a kind of windshield which was all the protection the brave passenger had if he was sitting in the third seat. The on-lookers of the time dubbed it "the mother-in-law's reserve".

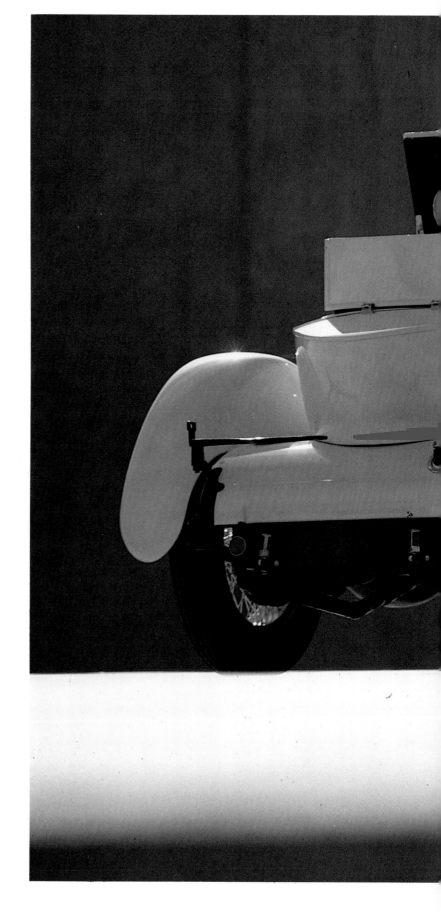

BALLOT 2LT
1926
And mother-in-law came, too

The first publicity for the Ghost went shamelessly to the point, stating quite simply "the best six-cylinder car in the world". That was in 1906. It was a century that fuelled its verve and culture on the desire to travel. Perfumes and good wines crossed the Atlantic, displaying old Europe's *art de vivre*. The only thing not on the ships was the automobile, but the Rolls soon came into vogue and all England was honoured. However, acknowledging this flower of British heritage was not free: each Rolls registered in the States was subject to customs duties of 45%, which was a lot of money even for such a royal prerogative. Brewster, a bodybuilder at Long Island and creator of the Rolls shown here, had bought several dozen chassis in 1907 and 1913. Then, in 1913, the Rolls-Royce bosses went over to the USA to suggest delivery or even manufacturing on site of "Rolls-Royce Eagle" engines because the Americans were less proficient in this field. It was stale-mate, but contact had been established and from 1920 a Rolls-Royce factory was set up in Springfield. Our Silver Ghost is in its own way an "American". It had six cylinders in line built on blocks of three cylinders which allowed it to cruise at 105 kph. Americans also introduced production lines because they could not understand why the gearboxes of the Ghost, which were completely handmade, should need 88 hours' work. The Ghost pictured here belonged to the Paramount studios and once, during the shooting of a film, had an unforgettable passenger: Jean Harlow.

14

ROLLS-ROYCE SILVER GHOST
PICCADILLY ROADSTER (BREWSTER)
1926

Ghosts like dollars, too

DELAGE D8 SS
(FERNANDEZ & DARRIN)
1930

A royal farewell

In 1874, thanks to its distilleries, the small town of Cognac had already acquired a solid worldwide reputation in the art of good-living. It was less well-known that Louise de Savoie, later duchess of Angouleme, gave birth here to one of the most famous kings of France: Francois the First. But that is not important; time has clouded over memory, and progress has made a clean breast of regrets.

The railways existed and Cognac had its station. The station, like any station, had a stationmaster and he, like any stationmaster, delegated the passage of trains and level crossing to a sub-stationmaster: Good Monsieur Delage. Louis Delage, his son, received civil status from the Lord Mayor of Cognac and one fine morning he showed once and for all that success has nothing to do with the lineage of a car.

In 1905, still very young, but a brilliant engineer, he built his first car. A little car to be precise, functioning thanks to the only decent French engine of the time, a De Dion-Bouton single cylinder of 1059 cc. In 1908 a Delage walked away with the ACF Grand Prix at Dieppe: no stops and an average of 80 kph—it was a fine win. Then, he won at Indianapolis, in 1914. The crowning achievement for Delage was in 1927 when the GP 1 500 cc car with a supercharger won all the grand prix of the season. A record which neither Ferrari nor Mercedes even in their heyday could have touched. Despite this very ample harvest of successes, Delage very coolly decided that, having nothing else to prove, he would stop competing in 1928. The racing cars were sold to private garages and from then on he had only one objective: the customer! In Delage's opinion there was someone somewhere dreaming of a car like the D8: a new model and the last model from the Delage company to leave the Salon de l'Automobile in Paris in 1929. The D8 was deliberately intended for wealthy clients. The eight-cylinder in-line engine of 4 060 cc, which developed 102 bhp at 3 500 rpm was installed on a long chassis with one of the most royal of bodies. On the other hand, for the D8S and the SS, a lighter and short chassis accommodated the same engine but with a higher compression ratio and a different camshaft. The D8 SS, which was essentially meant for the British market, was equipped with four SU carburettors with which the British importer guaranteed 160 kph.

This is a very fine model, with its body by Fernandez and Darrin, and belongs to the Automobile Museum at Mougins.

It was offered by the French government to Haili Selassi, Emperor of Ethiopia, on his coronation. King Gustav V paraded it in the Court of Sweden and Alexander of Jugoslavia was assassinated in Marseille on 9 October 1934 while driving a D8. In 1934 Delage was re-acquired by Hotchkiss with the money from cannon and other guns which he was manufacturing.

ROLLS-ROYCE PHANTOM II
(FONTAIN'S AUTO-CARRIAGE WORKS)
1930

A Phantom parry

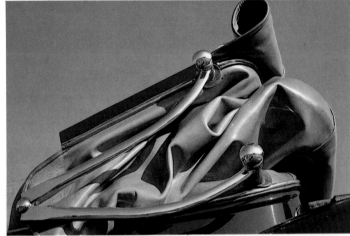

Legends, the fairies of history, bravely transcend time and the seasons, and the legend of Rolls-Royce is much the same. In reality the Rolls customer often rightly hesitated between the Cadillac, Isotta-Fraschini, Hispano-Suiza, Duesenberg, Pierce-Arrow and Mercedes—and the Phantom II, which was born of the need to parade before the invaders who were attacking from all directions, and whose advance Phantom II could not halt. Inheriting the old and venerable chassis of the Ghost, ill-treated by the excessively powerful engine, this model proved to be unable to bear the weight solely on its front brakes.

The only client moved to choose it out of love belongs to folklore as it was Nawab Wali-ud Dowla Bahadur, Head of State of Hyderabad. The Phantom II had to reawaken interest in the history

25

of the company and yet its era augured ill. It had an engine of 7 668 cc which drove it at 148 kph and not a kilometre more. No one at Rolls could get another horsepower out of the six-cylinder engine which had a modest 100 bhp. But as far as the chassis was concerned, things were in order. Inspired by the Twenty, the Phantom could keep its distance from its closest rivals—Bentley. Of course, listening contentedly to the royal purr of its engine was more important to the driver than deciding on where to go, but the compact Phantom II could also boast another advantage—that of the low weight/cost proportion as it weighed more than 2 490 kg. Also, no Hollywood star could claim to have a leather coat as well-fitting as its hood. Fitted by Fountain's Auto-Carriage Works it was as if each body was tailor-made for each car. Its first owner was unconcerned about its whims because he was one of the last professional poets to exercise the hobby of chasing butterflies.

PACKARD TWELVE SERIES II
CONVERTIBLE 1106
1934

The expensive Mirage

Packard built 8 000 cars in the United States in 1934. Of these, 960 were Twelves, the top-of-the-range version of the Packard which, since 1930, had been taking half of the world prestige market. The Twelve, however, was not born in happy circumstances. It was even a profession of blind faith as for four years the future was completely unknown. Nevertheless at the beginning of 1929 President Herbert Hoover, who had just been elected, made a speech: "Americans will soon be vanquishing poverty once and for all". It is true that from 1919 to 1929 industrial production increased by 64%. This prodigious leap was due to two sectors in particular: the construction and the automobile industries. What is more, at that time an estimated one person in five owned a car in the United States. Aided and abetted by forceful advertising, people were spending without doing

31

their accounts. Company profits soared between 1923 and 1929 by 62% whereas average wages increased by only 11%. The difference between production capacities and consumer spending power quickly became clear, as a result of the recession. On 11 December 1929 America was taken by surprise: the bank of the United States had not one dollar to its name and left behind it the ashes of the accounts of 500 000 of its clients—who were not the smallest at that. Automobile production was pulverised by the apocalyptic crash and fell by as much as 75% between 1929 and 1932. Each week 64 000 new jobless swelled the ranks of the legions of disaster. In 1933 there were 13 million jobless and in two years 2 300 banks had gone bankrupt. However, in the automobile sector people still tried their hand at new things, and proposed insolent luxury at a time when in everyday life people could barely buy the vital minimum. That was well and truly the end of the Packard Twelve. That large car which, when empty, weighed 2 417 kg, used an average of 26 litres per 100 km, and was being sold in 1934 with luxury extras for 4 425 dollars. Its V12, 7 292 cc engine was lubricated from a 9.5 litre tank. The circulating oil was cooled by a water capacity of 38 litres. All the tanks on this car were impressively sized, including the fuel tank which could take no less than 121 litres.

So much for the story of the car which has always been exaggeratedly unreasonable and privileged in its representation of a period. For a long time certain people had thought that better days to come would prove them right. Packard was convinced of the eternal nature of privilege and in the reality of mirages.

PANHARD 6 CS TYPE X 72
CABRIOLET "BELEN"
1934

Mr Kow's fantasy

This cabriolet is such a rare car that the only model known today is the one in the photograph. This gallant and debonair car, so naturally installed in its happy Parisian setting, was internationally conceived. Its valveless engine was developed from an idea by Knight Kilbourne, an American. The body is said to have been built from a design by Alexis Kow, a Russian sadly routed by the Revolution who yearned to one day exchange his pencil and his inexhaustible talent for a return to his two hectares of snow in the Ukraine. Circumstances did not allow him anything of the kind. Finally, Panhard, a French builder, would never have become famous if a German, Gottlieb Daimler, had not liked the marque as much as his country, so much so that he let a foreigner build the first car engine in the face of all opposition. Briefly, it was a strange crossbreed of international cerebral matter but also a wonderful show of open minds and of visions of the future rare in France at the time. . . .

This cabriolet is driven by a six-cylinder in-line engine with 2 516 cc whose foremost characteristic is that it is a valveless engine. An engine which has decided to do without the little disks on stalks which went feverishly back and forth, opening and shutting holes, allowing the gases to enter the cylinder head and then to escape. No-one could do better or knew how to change it, but the way it was posed certain problems. The valves took up space in the cylinder head which made it difficult to develop a better design for the efficiency of the combustion chamber. Also, working incessantly in an infernal heat, these valves ended up being "grilled" like tender vegetables in a casserole pot without oil. Knight Kilbourne investigated this and happened on placing between the cylinder and the

35

piston two sleeves which displaced each other alternatively and in which little holes, whose position was precisely calculated, allowed the gases to enter and escape. The valveless motor was born and from 1908 Panhard had been trying to adopt it.

This was only a beginning because this make was enlivened by the avant-garde. In a completely different context this curiosity in a brighter future expressed itself in Alexis Kow. This Russian is the man who at the beginning of the century revolutionised publicity design. Kow did not speak much, nor smile, but tossed ideas around in his head. Each of his posters projects fantasies which the car must respond to and the real design cannot satisfy. Alexis disturbed and amazed people by working for a long time on Panhard's graphics but was never satisfied until finally he perfected it. Kow wanted the design to be alive and mobile but also still quite feasible, as indeed this cabriolet is.

MERCEDES-BENZ 500 K
CABRIOLET B (SINDELFINGEN)
1935

Highroad courier

In the 1930s Mercedes-Benz already had an enviable list of race wins. In the range, apart from the SS, which had the double honour of being both fascinating and priceless (33 000 Reichsmarks, which took its 200 kph out of the reach of ordinary men), there was nothing convincing. So Mercedes began thinking and sketching, throwing away designs, redoing them and finally what was to be something of a cross between the unapproachable SS and the Mannheim Sport was conceived – a good little car although rather plagiarist. This new creation was the 380. At the Berlin Salon in 1933 it was the star. All the work had paid off: it was nobly finished, bewitchingly comfortable and solidly made—it registered a good 2 000 kilos on the weighing machine. To carry about two tonnes a large engine is obviously needed, and grafting a supercharger onto it was an even better idea. But at that time the supercharger and con-rods were not always well matched, especially with heavy-footed drivers. The 380 did not survive even a year. From then on Mercedes no longer discussed things, it demanded results: results alone counted, not opinions. The mishaps of the 380 had to be quickly forgotten. The 380 had barely started heading toward the museum when the 500 K appeared. It concealed an eight-cylinder engine managing 100 bhp or 160 bhp with a supercharger. This time it managed 216 kph, and its career was less fleeting as it kept its place in the catalogue until 1936. Despite everything it was a very rare car as only 354 models of the 500 K were ever made. The photograph shows a remarkably well preserved one attesting to a great moment in automobile industry

39

when the slightest error could prove fatal. The 500 K made up for the transient appearance of the 380 as certain versions were called "couriers of the highroads". The 540 K succeeded it and was the last representative of this noble lineage, of which only 12 models were built. It was now 1939 and German industry was called on to attend to a task completely different from building cars.

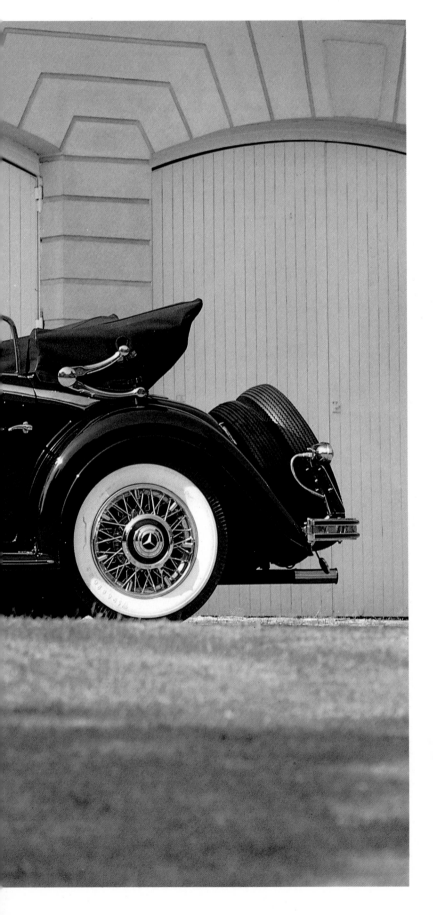

DELAHAYE 135 'COMPETITION' CABRIOLET (CHAPRON)

1936

Classical beauty

É mile Delahaye, who created the make, died in 1905. The man who took over as director of the company, Charles Weiffenbach, was a young engineer born in Thann at the foot of the Vosges. His Alsatian background gave him a solid fervour for seriousness and sturdiness which marked all the products of the company. Weiffenbach also diversified Delahaye—a diversification seriously needed. He conceived one of the first motorised carriages happily called "Tournesol". "Mr Charles", as he was nicknamed, also believed in consolidation, so from 1927 to 1932 Delahaye, Chenard and Walcker along with Rosengart who later joined, became business bedfellows, but without any worthwhile results.

In 1934 several young engineers worked at Delahaye on new ideas and Mr Charles often met with Ettore Buggati. The latter would only speak of high performance and competition cars. Bugatti was a talented lawyer and managed to talk Weiffenbach round to building the 134: an 18 horsepower car with six cylinders, which the following year was called the 135. That same year Delahaye bought Delage, which had a strong tradition in technology. Depending on the version, the Delahaye 135 could do between 145 and 165 kph. The 135 Competition featured here belongs to the Museum Vendée, some miles from Sables-d'Olone. This very fine car, with a six-cylinder 3.5-litre engine, could manage 120 bhp, was fed by three carburettors, measured four metres and weighed 935 kg. This Mylord cabriolet was designed by Henry Chapron, one of the great bodybuilders. At

45

about this time Figoni and Falschi, Langenthal, Franay, Guilloré, Labourdette, Dubos, Saoutchik, Letourneur, Marchan and Graber, inspired by the 135, all made cars where boldness was tinged with classical beauty—it was rare and exciting.

Developing the 135 engine gave Delage a place in competition history with René Dreyfus, Albert Divo, Louis Chiron, Eugène Chaboud and many others. From 1934 to 1954 more than 5 000 Delahayes were manufactured. Throughout the world 200 cars have been maintained of which 90% are 135s: a figure which testifies to the amazing spell this model cast on all who saw it.

49

ROLLS-ROYCE TWENTY
D.H.C. (SOUTHERN M.C.)
1936

A pretty masquerade

The construction of the Twenty had finally stopped in 1929 but seven years later this completely unrecognizable model, conceived in 1925, made an appearance on the market with the authority of something brand new. "Southern Motor Company" had passed by the same road. Reconditioning the chassis and modernising the body had given birth to a new model. Originally the Twenty was a small sensible car with a six-cylinder engine of more than three litres, and could just about exceed 100 kph. Quite a respectable speed in view of the fact that before 1925 it had brakes only on the back, of the shoe type. In this prewar period maharajas were rare and the Twenty had nothing special about it apart from the realistic simplicity of its manufacture. For purists it was no use weeping over the fortunate camouflage of the original version. It was common practice, and more than one chassis has been built with a town car body and another with a sports open tourer body, all easily interchangeable. In the United States in 1926 there was even a series of "Playboy" Rolls with a very obtrusive design assembled on a secondhand chassis: shocking.

51

Henry Ford—the creator of the Ford Motor Company in 1903—was a countryman and ruthless with it. In his mind, that of a farmer's son, there was all the logic behind his fantastic success. For as many models of a car as possible to sell, as many people as possible have to be able to buy. Before it came of age, he had heralded the coming of the popular car. And that was the Ford T. Fifteen million cars in this range came out between 1908 and 1927 and brought in lots of dollars. The Ford A (four and a half million examples) took over from 1927 to 1932, but Ford, who stubbornly believed in the unique car, found himself up against a competition which was offering a wider choice: that was the birth of the V8 series. The eight cylinders in line was common enough, but its bulkiness prevented it being housed under small bonnets. With this choice of V8 the upper range of the average car was born and remained almost unique to Ford until the eve of the Second World War. The V8 range was a programme in itself as it came in 14 models, one of which is this pretty cabriolet.

FORD V8–78
CLUB CABRIOLET
1937

V8 for the masses

The Peugeot 402 was the basis for this strange mechanical bodywork. Essentially, it was composed of a solid metal roof which could be removed simply and without any fuss and put in the boot with the use of curious stylised tools.

The inventor was Georges Paulin, who was neither an engineer nor a bodybuilder but even more oddly a dentist.

Paulin soon abandoned his practitioner's chair once and for all because a short time earlier he had met Marcel Pourtout, a bodybuilder from Rueil. Georges Paulin received advice and guidance and actually listened to it, managing to forge his own style. The 402 Darl'Mat of which over 100 examples were built was surely the best guarantee of this talent from elsewhere. As for the genius idea of the removable solid hood, well, it ended up having a fairly modest career. In fact if there were a crash from behind, which even happened in those days, the boot had to be readjusted along with the hood it housed. That is if the owner did not have to buy a new one.

From the outset in the short history of this special make an electrical switch controlled the metamorphosis of this curious steel chrysalid. The mechanism was costly, did not last long and its futuristic character failed when faced with the cruel reality of a flat battery.

However, what was special in this "transformable" is that it still remains one of the boldest and most beautiful bodies in automobile history.

PEUGEOT 402L
ELECTRIC TRANSFORMER
1937

Mr Paulin's chrysalid

HISPANO-SUIZA K6
(KELLNER)
1937

The graceful Stork

The Company, Hispano-Suiza Fabrica de Automoviles, was set up in 1906 in Barcelona and, as its name suggests, was a Swiss-Spanish concern. The Swiss contribution was in the form of the nationality of the founder, Mark Birkigt, a brilliant engineer if ever there was one. In 1914 he was the father of what is still considered the best aeroplane engine of the First World War. With 50 000 of this model built this motor was a strongpoint of SPAD aircraft manufactured by Bleriot. If the stork was still on the Hispano radiator it was because the flight of the stork, the *cicogne* in French, commanded by Captain Guynemer, was equipped with a SPAD when he was brought down at 23 years of age on 11 January 1917 above Poelkapelle in Belgium. Georges Guynemer achieved his 54th victory in this combat, but history will only remember his disappearance as a puzzle since neither his machine, "Old Charlie", nor his body were ever found.

War stories apart, from 1908 Hispano set up in Courbevoie, France. In 1919 the company launched the H6 which was incontestably the most fascinating car of the time. The engine was a six-cylinder in-line but the cylinder head, the connecting rods and pistons were quite similar to those of an aeroplane engine. This engineering was admired in its time as befitted the finest of engines. The chassis is also very much state of the art. It left anything Cadillac or even Rolls-Royce made technically far behind. The 1930 crisis did not affect the

solid reputation of the H6 but companies had to be realistic and rapidly think of reducing production costs. The K6 is in a certain way a response to this need. Aesthetically it is simpler and shows the realism adopted in its rejuvenation. This time it adopts an inverted motor of 4 900 cc—less noble, of course, but lighter and still a six-cylinder. Kellner, who was Birkigt's favourite bodybuilder—he had already been seen dressing a Buggatti Royale—yet again achieved wonders with the K6, showing his perfectionist's instinct for a work of art.

HORCH 853A
SPORT-CABRIOLET
1938

The ceremonial bunker

In 1937 Germany, was a little strange. Doctor August Horch, however, who was building cars during the day and dreaming about them at night was not at all strange. However, the parades and brass bands induced him to fantasise about a strange car. True, he said to himself, a car which can sport an official plate or even better the flag of a Head of State, a car for parading in, is much more impressive than one which just drives along. Dr Horch also had some old accounts to settle with Mercedes which thought it could do anything it liked when it came to putting on a show. Paradoxically, the 853 is a kind of answer to that, even though August Horch was a very ordinary person. In fact, from 1896 to 1899 he was a mechanic at Benz, which was a serious business. But, perhaps, not serious enough for him, as something motivated him to go and settle in Cologne so as to build his first car. He built engines from 1 600 to 6 500 cc and experienced the same passion for all engines. After that 6, 8 and 12 cylinders all flew from his designer's pencil with the same cool reasoning. The 853 is a perfect illustration of this. This is not a car calculated to suit the driver, it was for the dignitary it was carrying. It gives the unique feeling of imagining the road passing under the wheels without the car even moving forward. This car has a fear of breaking down; as proof, four hydraulic jacks allowed it to raise each wheel separately and instantaneously. This philosophy was also present in that it had on board a greasing pump which lubricated the chassis without the driver having to

67

get out of the car. Finally, there was the gearbox, whose every ratio was raised to adopt a quiet cruising speed on the motorway. Also fascinating is that this car weighed 2 650 kg without a drop of oil or petrol.

Well, what is there to say about the technology which refused to take the slightest risk with the engine? Eight cylinders in line and 120 bhp for a five-litre engine, 135 kph top speed. The Horch 853 was the first bunker-on-wheels before its time!

CITROËN 11B
CABRIOLET
1938

Good breeding

The 11, as the French called it from its first day, appeared in the Citroën catalogue of autumn 1934, but in that same year the cabriolet 7 was already being manufactured and was marketed until 1939. It was developed in the front-wheel-drive range and deserves not to be forgotten. In fact from 1935 the 11 Légère version took over from the 7 Sport, while the cabriolet 11 Normale had a happy existence. In 1937 it was baptised the 11B for simplicity's sake. The main difference between the 11 Normale and 11 Légère was in the tracking, the axle base and the width of the body.

Like most of its siblings, the Citroën cabriolet was not rigid, so when driving at speed over a nightmarish road surface its stability gave some cause for concern. This is why it was not retained in the top performance range because, apart from two prototypes, there was no cabriolet version of the 15.

To get back to the Cabriolet 11B, it had all leather seats in colours matching the body. And, oddly, the cabriolet's indicators next to the doors were only fitted as an extra on the principle that the driver or his passenger could easily stretch out an arm when they were turning. The customers rarely complained. These customers were relatively well-off and excellent business for the accessorists when their cabriolet was delivered. Fancy radiators, all manner of lights, radio, cacophonic horns which were not often very melodious, nothing was too beautiful, nor too ostentatious for the buyer. The theft of these cars was considered easier than that of the classic saloon, so owners would often procure a sort of antitheft bar which locked the steering-wheel if they did not use the gear stick. As far as its performance went, this model could reach 120 kph but the testers of the time were relatively cautious on this subject for, as we mentioned, the lack of a metal hood considerably reduced the rigidity of the body and driving at high speeds was not advisable too often.

71

It was a day much like any other, when Ettore Arco Isodoro Bugatti, a famous car maker, decided to marry Barbara Mascherpa Bolzoni, no less than the great singer at the Scala of Milan. It was commonly felt that it was high time because Barbara, before saying "yes" to the Mayor, had already agreed with great happiness and natural sobriety to bear Ettore's three children. The first was Jean, who was born on 20 January 1909 in Cologne. From the age of 20 Jean, already car-crazy, began to design bodies for Bugatti. The young man rightly thought that his father often had grand ideas which had little to do with commercial reality and began thinking of a car which was more commonplace, more of a town car, but also more brilliant in its compactness: obviously the Bugattis were genii but they also lacked something. This was the 57. Obviously to leave a mark of his authority, Ettore senior was going to keep the principle of the rigid front axle. Finally, it was "ready for the Salon" and the 57 was exhibited in Paris in 1933. With its eight-cylinder in-line engine and double camshaft everyone agreed it was admirably suited to prolonging the Bugatti tradition. In 1936 300 Bugatti "57 type" were built and it had to be admitted that certain changes were desirable. The chassis was reinforced and the engine mounted on four rubber blocks. It also gained a twin choke carburettor and a new crankcase which permitted fitting a supercharger. This supercharger was offered as an optional that next year and with it the car had between 135 and 160 bhp and gained 20 kph on its top speed: a neat 170 kph. This transform-

BUGATTI 57 SC
DROPHEAD COUPÉ (CORSICA)
1938

The supercharged Corsican

ation also changed its name to a 57C, and what had to happen happened.

In August 1936 the 57 begot a sports version. With lowered, shorter chassis and higher compression ratio the 57S found it difficult to persuade people: too docile and tender, and it needed a supercharger. Thus we got the "SC", 200 bhp and 200 kph. Dandies had to make room for real men, but the model was out of the range required by professional pilots and in 1938 production was halted. Thirty odd models were produced, but of course this rareness made collectors only value it more. Often the body was built by Gangloff, Van den Plas, Van Vooren and finally Corsica, which is the case with this fine example kept in an exceptional state by the Automobilists' Museum. Later the 57 engendered the "tank", an engine essentially destined for competition in which Jean Bugatti died during a test drive at 10.00 am on 11 August 1939 between Molsheim and Strasbourg. Sixteen years previously Jean Bugatti had wanted the 57 to be first and foremost a safe and civilised car, but Heaven, a drunken cyclist and a tree decided otherwise.

TALBOT LAGO T150SS
CABRIOLET (FIGONI & FALASCHI)
1938

Curved air

The history of Talbot is rather like that of a powder store, or an arsenal where, between explosions, as if nothing had happened, it is built bigger, higher and finer. Perhaps optimism is also madness but a good dose of it was necessary all at one go to conceive this car and to negotiate with the bankers the postponement to a later date of the end of an era. Anthony Lago, the boss of Talbot, was made just that way. It is true that in this year, when Figoni made the body of the surprising T150SS, Anthony Lago had just turned 45 and already had the reputation of a tough fighter. From his Venetian birth he kept the romanticism of turbulent passions, and the passion he put into each of his cars could not be more so. He was called the "major". It was in fact the grade of the engineer from the Polytechnic of Milan at the end of the war in 1918 for which the Italian army had enrolled him. As soon as he got out of his uniform he went to England and became responsible for the distribution of the Isotta-Fraschini. After many trials and tribulations in several companies busying themselves with the car he became director general in 1934 of the Talbot car company at Suresnes. Unwearying, he cleaned up, reorganised, demanded and suggested things to this business which was up to its neck in all sorts of trouble. That same year, the T range appeared at the Salon of Paris. The 150 version was a completely new model. Anthony Lago had to literally promote the company he had just taken over. The T150 was the vehicle of his ambition. It was equipped with a sumptuous six cylinders with 2996 cc which, with a unique carburettor managed 110 bhp at 4 000 rpm. Two brand new regal cabriolets had the honour of being placed on the stand. In the catalogue Talbot specified that the maximum speed was 150 kph with an average consumption of 20 litres per 100 km.

In 1936, torpid Talbot was on the edge of a precipice and Anthony Lago filed a petition for bankruptcy, but he was as solid as a rock. He wanted a new style for Talbot, a quicker commercial pace, and he would have all that. In a good year, 30 different models were registered in the catalogue, despite the lack of money and never-ending in-fighting in the company. The T150 was developed and had a four-litre engine. It was called SS, for Super Sport, and in England that allowed it to be referred to as "Short Special". The chassis

81

fitted with its engine weighed 850 kg and according to the gear ratios the SS drove at between 160 and 180 kph. From 1937 Lago entrusted the bodies to Figoni but the latter was completely free to create whatever his pencil thought fit on the base of the T150. In the month of May 1938, this cabriolet came from his pencil.

Almost 50 years later you can still see mobs of people around this car, transfixed. People stare and not a finger moves. The onlookers, witnesses to the conquest of the moon, dream of another planet on which this motorised body could be driven. Surely not ours.

This Lagonda LG6 had a 4.5-litre engine and was the first car in this range to have such an engine.

This M45 model was a six-cylinder with overhead valves and was conceived and built in a time which will no doubt remain a record in the great world of cars. Indeed, research into the LG6 started in 1933 and this car was marketed the following year. Then the style and the engine were developed, soon putting it into the highest of classes. In fact in 1934 the M45 had, after certain transformations, become the M45R and the engine which the "Rapide" version was equipped with won the 24 Hour Race at Le Mans in 1935. And what a win! The course had 58 cars at the start but only 28 made it to the finish and, although the Lagonda 4 451 cc piloted by H S Hindmarsch and L Fontes managed to cover 3 006.7 km in 24 hours at an average speed of 125.2 kph it was only 8.4 km ahead of its nearest pursuer. Much too close again, because without knowing it the winning team had set off for Le Mans just a few days before Lagonda went into liquidation. The firm had been under financial pressure for some time. Sadly, reality put paid to one of the most beautiful works in the history of the Lagonda.

However, the technological potential, like the company name, made taking over Lagonda a profitable business. Rolls-Royce was attracted and competed but too late: Alan Good managed to sign the take-over. He wanted to give a breath of life to

LAGONDA LG6
DROPHEAD COUPÉ
1938

The road from Le Mans

Lagonda and Walter Owen Bentley's name was running through his mind: the famous name of an English engineer who was the most talented man of his generation. For Alan Good he was the only man capable of realizing this desire for change at Lagonda without ruining his prestigious acquisition.

Getting *carte blanche*, W O Bentley accepted the post as Technical Director at Lagonda, and by 1936 his influence was already affecting company production. It was to show even more clearly in the completeness of the LG6 of 1938 and many other cars.

That evening the crowds had bustled into the cinema so as not to miss *Quai des brumes*, a romantic film by Marcel Carne. One couple, Michele Morgan and Jean Gabin were selling yet again the story of eternal love. The auditorium had saved up all its tears. About midnight, strong gusts of wind had taken over from a weak north wind, which could not even pull the last leaves from the trees. The last drinks had been consumed at Fouquet's. The beginning of autumn in 1938 was saturated with nostalgia. Several days previously, on 30 September in Munich, the meeting between Chamberlain, Daladier, Mussolini and Hitler had ended in fiasco. None of the participants had opposed the German claims on Czechoslovakia. The irreparable was becoming irreversible. However, good news allowed engineering buffs to smile: Teflon had been industrialised. It was a plastic material prepared from tetrafluoroethylene enabling joints to be made which were resistant to high temperatures, corrosion and even harmful chemical agents. And then in mid-week, the Paris Automobile Salon opened its doors. And what a show! A whole spectacle of novelties: the Simca 8, the Renault Juvaquatre, the Peugeot 202 and the Rosengart *Supercinq*. And then there were all the others which people were looking at, convincing themselves that dreams were not merely for the young. Several days later, all the visitors stood around the Delahaye 165 stand amazed. Who was this car for and why was it built? In its catalogue Delahaye stated very clearly and directly in the heading, without the slightest tone of contempt: "For the Elite". The reputation of the man who built it was known. In Delahaye's range, well-

DELAHAYE 165
(FIGONI & FALASCHI)
1938

For the elite

known for its sports cars the whole world over, there was no model able to outclass Maybach, Rolls-Royce, Horch, Bugatti, Lagonda, Mercedes, Alfa Romeo or even Delage, his compatriot. From 1937 Delahaye had mastered the V12 with 4.5 litres, which had to comply with international regulations applying from the following year to cars which we could call the Formula 1s of the time. This fine piece of engineering weighed over 268 kg and had 235 bhp—on its good days. After numerous modifications, it quickly became successful. This Delahaye 165 is in some way derived from this, but is of much higher class. Every professional driver wanted one. The Delahaye 165 is a rare collector's jewel because parts were only intended to be made for 12 cars: five were made. They were the pride and joy of the master body-builders, with Giuseppe Figoni leading them. The Delahaye 165 is one of the finest stars in this story which inspired romanticism, adventures and even folly: the Shah of Iran ordered an identical one—from Bugatti.

This car was reminiscent of the 1950s but in fact was launched in 1936. Despite the crisis of the time, apart from Chevrolet and Ford, who were very sure of their four-cylinder engines, most manufacturers thought that the reputation of a car was proportional to the number of its cylinders. Cadillac with its V16 was leading this mad challenge. Lincoln did not lag behind surprisingly because for a long time this marque had always been pursued by the big car monopoly. In 1932 a 7.2 litre V12 engine entered the Lincoln range. This engine was also important as, until 1948, all Lincolns had a V12 engine. Previously, in 1934 the competition, amazed, realised that Lincoln had manufactured an engine of 6.8 litres with an aluminium cylinder head. The engine, revolutionary for its time, allowed the leader of the marque to go at 165 kph. But in 1934 the decline set in. For some time people tried to control their impatience and waited for the hard times to go away, but the cruel Depression had arrived. Then Lincoln launched the Zephyr, aiming to offer an economical car which maintained the illusion of the golden dream which Hollywood still continuously poured out. Technically the model was very simple. Its 4 380 cc V12 engine was considered in 1938 as a carefully thought out engine slightly more powerful than the Ford V8 whose chassis and gearbox the Zephyr borrowed. Even though its speed of approximately 150 kph was acceptable, its

LINCOLN ZEPHYR
CONVERTIBLE COUPÉ
1938

Shoestring dream

acceleration was fairly sluggish. The velvety hum of the engine punctuated by an exhaust with flat tones was a subtle invitation for royal rides of quiet detachment. They made the driver feel relaxed, which was understandable as the brakes were trustworthy and efficient.

With the Zephyr, Lincoln was presaging another crisis which would be coming 50 years later.

The 2500S came out in 1939. But suffering had doused curiosity, and people's thoughts were not on cars. Happy and carefree Italy shuddered, as the war was in full flow. But the Superleggera had personality. First, the flattering spells of a beautiful six-cylinder in-line engine with 2 443 cc, and then its body by Touring: a guarantee of originality which left a mark on the life of the founder of this company, Felice Bianchi Anderloni. Being a lawyer and an aristocrat, he should by rights not have found himself in metalwork, but he belonged to a large family and three of his sisters married the founders of a great make of the time: Isotta Fraschini. Felice, in spite of himself, took an interest in this milieu burning with new-found passion but never sure of what tomorrow would bring. He was won over and quickly revealed that he could be an excellent test driver. In the group there were some rough hearties like the Maserati brothers, but Fate had other things in store for him. His glasses carefully placed on his marble–white pure nose, his pocket fastened with the shape of a royal pin, carnations in his lapel, he began to direct the Company Peugeot Italienne, issuing instructions for a new body after his own style for the tiny Peugeot open tourer Sport of 720 cc. In 1926, at 44, he made up his mind: he would be a coachbuilder. It marked the birth of Touring which would build car bodies which were in a class of their own, like Sala, Castagna and Farina.

ALFA ROMEO 2500S
CABRIOLET 4 POSTI (TOURING)
1939

Avanti Anderloni

CHRYSLER C-39
TOWN AND COUNTRY
1949

Wurlitzer on wheels

Well before the last war motorways were already too limited for the American cars' fantasies and extravagances to express themselves, as they were intended to by their very nature and inspiration. Consequently, the Woodies were born in a very limited series. These cars were clad in wood so that the steel would only be a support. It was an invitation to go hunting and fishing, as good a reason as any which advertisers could plug.

This folly inevitably doled out the inconveniences of its wild excesses equally between the client and maker. Wood had to be found, dry but still alive enough to work on days of insistent rain or on a scorching summer's day; not to mention the difficulty of fitting this fiendishly difficult inlaid work. Each model was worked on by hand during the fitting stage. And what conviction the skilled labourer invested, almost free of charge, in plating the royal fibre of Honduras mahogany on a plate of ash. For the owner, the compromise between the delicately exotic and the solidly rustic was not of course without its limitations. Regular careful varnishing was needed to keep intact the woodwork's shining rustic effect and this needed an equally unusual devotion: for example, note the colour of this Woodie: Sumac red. Of all the many species of Sumac, the *Rhus Vernicefera* is lovingly cultivated for its secretions of a juice necessary to make Japan varnish which is spread on Woodies.

107

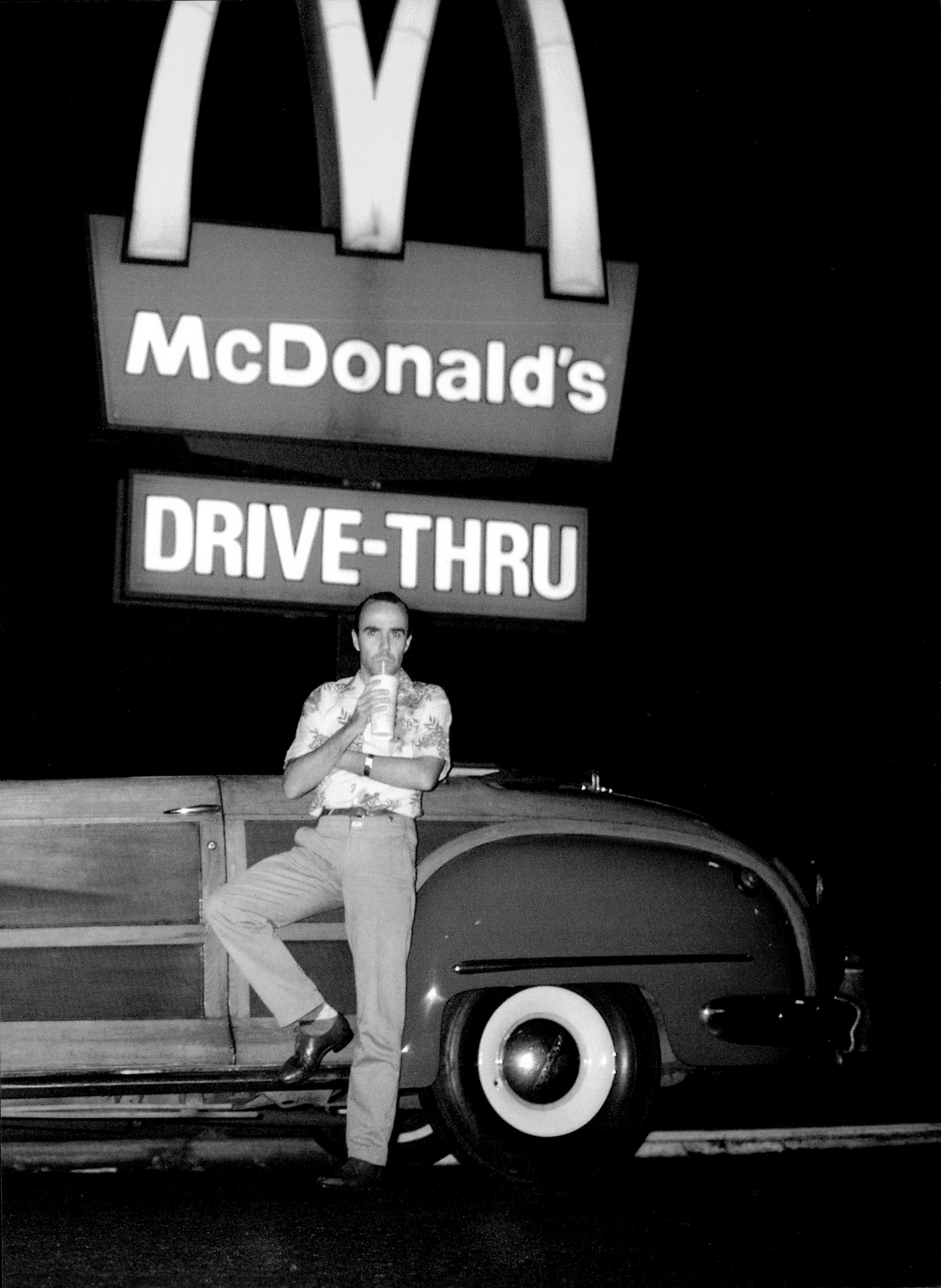
McDonald's
DRIVE-THRU

Rolls-Royce, Aston Martin and Lagonda will never forget all that Walter Owen Bentley succeeded in bringing to their makes' image. He was not like Ford or Louis Renault, a pioneering DIY car buff covered in grease. He was a gentleman by birth, education and nature. His cars were always solemn without being pompous, refined but without any pretensions. This cabriolet, whose body was built by Park Ward, had six cylinders with 4 253 cc over which hung two SU carburettors. Bentley, youngest in a family of nine children, started his career in the railways, as an engineer. He looked at cars but that was all, even though his finances permitted him to buy the most beautiful cars of the day. Timidly, he started competing, but he was always toying with his engines, preparing them, improving them. But then, at the railways, the salary was distressingly modest, even if the higher echelons had many privileges. So Bentley accepted a position as a director of the maintenance service in a taxi company. At 24 years of age, with one of his brothers, he imported several makes of French cars, of which one was the DFP. He improved on it and fitted it with aluminium pistons. The First World War arrived, Bentley did his military duties and concentrated on airplane engines. From 1919 to 1931 he founded his own make of car before being bought up by Rolls-Royce, after which he was the man with great verve at Lagonda and Aston Martin. He died in 1971 at 83. The history book of the English car owes him its greatest pages.

BENTLEY MARK VI
DROPHEAD FOURSOME COUPÉ (PARK WARD)
1949

The gentleman

JAGUAR MARK V
DROPHEAD COUPÉ
1950

Old and new

At the beginning of 1901 England was turning over a new page. "The grandmother of Europe", Queen Victoria, who had been reigning over a world of 390 million subjects expired in her Osborne castle. In that same year William Lyons was born, the son of a piano dealer. On his 21st birthday rather than going to drink with his mates in his local to celebrate his coming of age, he started his first company and became, as a matter of course, the founder of Jaguar. Of all the strange stories of the company, that of the Mark V stands out. For the London exhibition of 1948, William Lyons had got away from the rigidity of his normal chassis. He wanted to make a break, to create both a change in its design, and a serious mechanical development. Unfortunately the new design of the body brought in panels which were too large to be made at Jaguar until the following year, and sub-contracting would have been financially disastrous. To put paid to everything, the production of the new engine caused problems as difficult as those caused by the body. Innovation had to know its limits. Thus, the Mark V was born on a very traditional body with old style elegance. It sold well for two years but was one of the Jaguars missing that spark of vitality.

It looks a little timid for an American, almost afraid; doubtless, because from 1966 this car was an orphan. In fact that year Studebaker definitively closed its doors having been associated for more than ten years with Packard. Henry and Elem Studebaker, the founders, were builders of horse carriages. Soon, the cars of that make made a name for themselves because of their reliability, their very reasonable maintenance cost and their almost popular cost price. After the Second World War, like Cadillac, aviation inspired designers. But this time it was the radiator in the form of an aircraft propellor which was endowed with this grace from the Heavens. In the history of the firm one of the finest models remained the Studebaker 53, very harmoniously sketched by a Frenchman, Raymond Loevy, apostle of what the Americans were soon to be calling "Design". The Champion was fitted with a six-cylinder in-line engine and reached an acknowledged respectable speed of 150 kph. The hood control was electrical and for the first time for Studebaker this car had automatic transmission.

118

STUDEBAKER CHAMPION
REGAL CONVERTIBLE
1951

Quiet American

ASTON MARTIN DB 2
DROPHEAD COUPÉ
1952

A fast start

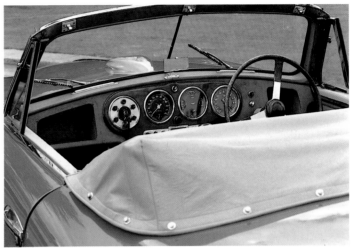

In 1914 Lionel Martin, a very wealthy Englishman, had been putting together a racing car and won with it at the race at Aston-Clinton. It is the matching of these two names which created Aston Martin. When peace returned, Martin decided to become a car builder. But after making 50 cars of a prototype he had been working on since 1920 he no longer had any money and gave up the business. Aston Martin had two owners before the interval imposed by the Second World War because of financial troubles. Then, in 1947, Aston Martin made a fresh start, the beginning of an ambition of global dimensions which cut the work out for other long-established companies. The man who assumed the task was an industrialist, both young and rich. In his ambitious stride, several months later, he also became owner of Lagonda. And then David Brown got down to work. Out came the DB 1 (for David Brown). In fact, it was merely the grafting of old solutions onto one another and this adulterous offshoot could not even lay claim to belong to the same family as the DB 2, to which it bequeathed only inspiration for the chassis and the suspension.

Lagonda had inherited a six-cylinder 2.5 litre engine with superb overhead camshafts. Conceived by W O Bentley, after being fettled, it became the pride and joy of Aston Martin for nigh on 25 years. Several prototypes of the DB 2 were registered at the 24 Hour Race at Le Mans in 1949, of which one was fitted with a six-cylinder engine. That was the first car to come out after the war. It was an important event as the President of France, Vincent Auriol, himself went to Le Mans. On the sixth lap disaster struck, when the water pump began to leak and the race was given up. So, now the company concentrated on the customer version which had to be ready for the London Car Show in 1950. At that time Great Britain used low grade petrol and this regal piece of engineering had to adopt a lower compression ratio, reducing power to 105 bhp. Less than a year later, things were put right and the DB 2 Vantage range had 125 bhp at its disposal. At the end of 1950, 100 copies of this cabriolet were built and for three years of the DB 2's existence they accounted for a quarter of its sales. Not so bad!

LINCOLN CAPRI SPECIAL CUSTOM CONVERTIBLE

1954

Queen of Sierra Madre

America discovered the Capri in 1952. At first sight it looked like any other Lincoln, but its engineers, who had been busying themselves for three years on a very dull range, made a big effort this time.

In particular they had replaced the large 5 526 cc flat configuration engine which Lincoln used until then for its cars, and Ford, the owner of the company, used for his lorries! Today it is a superb V8 with overhead valves. This was a classy piece of engineering, so much so that after 20 years' absence Ford decided that the Capri could and should underwrite the firm's return to competition. From 1952 the Capri was lined up in the Carrera Panamericana: over 3 200 kms, a course full of sun and folly which starts north of the Sierra Madre in Mexico and goes to Tuxtla, full of volcanic lava and perched at 2 000 metres. In 1952 the Capri took the first five places in the Tour series and Stevenson again in 1953. In 1954 it was goodbye to the Panamericana. The Capri went from 160 to 205 bhp, but the Ferrari of Maglioli was unbeatable even though Crawford and Faulkner won their category. The Lincoln Capri won its laurels as a great competitor. Its buyers and history would take this into account.

When you think of France in the postwar 1950s you perhaps think of a picture of Epinal, with luxury making a comeback: Cartier, Balmain, Dom Perignon. It was the era of Jean Daninos who looked like an English lord, lacking only a moustache and a few inches. He decided that the automobile industry owed this rediscovered prestige a car. Then at the end of 1951 Jean Daninos, who had already founded the Forges and Ateliers de Construction d'Eure-et-Loire (Facel), prepared the design of a prototype. But Facel as a name for his car was too short, too common. He asked his brother, Pierre, who was the author of a famous book—*Major Thompson's Diaries*—to help him find this first name. Pierre was more sensitive to dreaming about stars than perversities of engines and suggested choosing the name of a star. Thus it was—Véga. The star is in the constellation of the Lyre which in summer, at our latitude, can be seen for about 22 hours. Véga is 26 light years away from the earth and 50 times brighter than the sun. So much imagination and romanticism just for a car. At the close of 1951 the first part of the Véga project was being completed. It was a 2+2 coupé. The form of the model was already being etched in Jean Daninos' mind, but the engine was still the unknown factor. No French engine appealed to him. Alfa Romeo was a solution but the Italians were not too interested in this kind of collaboration. He became impatient to find one

128

FACEL-VÉGA/FVS/FV1
CABRIOLET
1955

A passing star

and logically looked towards the United States, which he knew well since the war. Chrysler Corporation let him freely select one of the prolific family of V8 engines. Daninos thus had a modern group because for five years Chrysler had been working on the second generation of V8 engines, which would resemble those with side valves. After studying the entire range Jean Daninos settled on a De Soto Firedome. It was endowed with more than 4 500 cc and it could manage 180 bhp and would give the Facel a speed of about 195 kph. The engine was tested for a long time. The car was tested day and night and little by little the report schedule allowed the last requirements which made the Facel a very special car: seven layers of paint with a completely leather interior. Nothing was omitted in the cause of surprise, value and delight.

In 1954 the Véga was finally discovered by the public. It was a year when France was sure it would never be at war again. In May, after 55 days of resistance shared by the whole world, the last bastion of France in Vietnam fell.

The Véga was a success. In 1955 a convertible model was brought out and was admired by everyone—which was a rare enough phenomenon; everyone, that is, apart from Daninos because this cabriolet was a real source of worry to him. In fact, as it needed special tools, the model disturbed the organisation of the coupé line. Moreover, as with almost all the cabriolets of this generation, the Véga was not rigid enough. At high speeds it was very noisy and shook so much that it displayed doubtful stability. Jean Daninos stopped building it after only seven models—which is why it is such a valuable collectors' piece.

130

The century was now half-way through. Wars were over and all Europe was pretending to forget about them. At BMW, however, this proud optimism resulted in the worst! The 501 was marketed in November 1952 without market research or regard for the competition. Of course, it had a standard radio but was marked at 15 100 Marks, which at the time was a veritable fortune. However, the Mercedes 220, a powerful car of almost historical stature was on sale for 12 000 Marks, and the Opel Kapitän, solidly bourgeois with its reputation for sturdiness and finish, cost only 9 000 Marks to buy. It was all but a disaster, with the repercussions creating a storm.

In 1955 it was felt that the Head of State should have a BMW as an official car with the bodywork by Michelotti. Konrad Adenauer, however, let it discreetly be known that he preferred his Mercedes 300. It was a difficult situation what with Germany waking up each morning with loving, but mistrusting eyes for Mercedes, and the United States the same, where Jaguar was having a run of bad luck. BMW was not entirely stuck, however, because Max Hoffman, the importer, was in the United States. He was a strange man, a motivated, ambitious person who was also as sly as an old fox. For a long time now he had been looking for a real car with real prestige. Max knew Count Albrecht Goertz, an industrial designer who in his free-time

BMW 507
TOURING SPORT ROADSTER
1956

Bavarian master work

was into designing cars. Hoffman gave Goertz the go-ahead, and soon the 503 had been etched: a 2+2 deriving from the 502. But yet again, the factory was locked into its fixed ideas and could not free itself from certain production limitations. The sides were much flatter than on the original design and it weighed 1 500 kg. Goertz was displeased and made no attempt to hide it. He was allowed to continue, and developed the 503, or as it turned out the 507. The light alloy body was lower and built on a tubular chassis which meant that it weighed no more than 1 330 kg. The V8, 3 168 cc engine had an extra ten horsepower and managed 150 bhp at 5 000 rpm. The 507 was on offer with three different axle ratios and, depending on the version selected, the car had a top speed of between 190 and 220 kph. Elvis Presley amongst others sat at the steering wheel and Hans Stuck drove it with great success on a hill-climb course.

All the factory technicians adored it like a child, but nonetheless the 507 was only produced for three years, which explains why only 252 specimens were built—much to the chagrin of collectors.

LANCIA AURELIA GT 2500
CONVERTIBLE B24S (PININFARINA)
1956

Roman road

Gianni Lancia, Vincenzo's son, was the founder of the make, and was 30 years old when building of the prototype of the Aurelia B24S cabriolet was completed. He was immediately enamoured with it and made it his personal car. Of course, Gianni could have had even more impressive cars, so it was a good sign. Aurelia had youth under her bonnet in the shape of concise inspiration by Pininfarina, where the manly form was sometimes curved to give the idea of gentle caresses. The engine was the beautiful V6 of the B20 with 2 451 cc. In 1955 the cabriolet was ready. All that remained was to find a name evoking escape without limit: and that was Aurelia. The name is taken from one of the most important Roman roads in Italy, as it left the Gate of Janicula and finished at Antipolis (Antibes) in Gaul. It followed the Mediterranean and crossed Civita Vecchia, Pisa and Genoa. The Lancia Aurelia, in spite of its very Latin civil status, was destined, to everyone's surprise, to seduce the United States to such a degree that a whole series was baptised "America". Lancia was amazed by its success. Surprises from the automobile industry often elude market research, as in other areas. At the same time the Old World was developing a taste for Coca Cola.

The Second World War was over, and America was at a loss for things to do. At Cadillac production started up again with large elongated "chocolate box" cars. Nostalgia wed anonymity, and Harley Earl, who for a long time had been deciding everything at Cadillac, confided in his collaborators. It was one of those situations where the fleeting spontaneity of flashes of genius can profit from a child's naivety.

Harley Earl had seen a fighter at an airport—a star of air fights of the war which people already wanted to forget about. This plane was the Lockheed Lightning P38, whose silhouette was characterised by a particularly slender and protracted fuselage. Adapting this technique to the automobile, in addition to the fact that it did not improve on the aerodynamics, seriously complicated the requirements of the production process. But in his mind, Harley had already fixed long ailerons onto the next Cadillacs: from 1948, until the 62 in 1959—a record, no-one would be able to beat. This model, the war horse of Cadillac, apart from its 325 bhp was a variation of all the fantasies of the buyers. In fact, they could choose two combinations from eight different colours of leather. As for the hood, which of course was electrically controlled, it gave the choice of five shades, each louder than the other. Bad taste could be accounted for.

CADILLAC 62
CONVERTIBLE COUPÉ
1959

Flight of fancy

JAGUAR XK150
DROPHEAD COUPÉ
1959

Everyman's cat

In 1957 the news on the world scene called for two events to be remembered: the launching of the Sputnik 1 by the Russians and that of the Jaguar XK150 by the English. The appearance of this new model created a storm amongst conservatives of the make. Jaguar had wanted to make a less marked, less élitist car than the famous XK120 and 140 so as to open the field to more customers but they were accused of having done nothing more than give these two models a face-lift. Purists had reason to grumble. The burr walnut had disappeared from the console and, even more scandalous, the door panels were imitation. Another innovation, the famous leaping jaguar, was offered as an option and from 1956 onwards the feline mascot on the bonnet had its back paws stretched as if to pounce as opposed to folded back. The XK150, at 1570 kg, was also the heaviest of the Jaguar cars. But even so it was successful, as in October 1960 on the last day of production 2671 models had been built. Its XK engine, with six cylinders and double overhead camshafts, reached 190 or 210 bhp depending on the type, and its all-steel body had a bonnet and boot in aluminium. This Jaguar which was meant to "please the whole world" managed at least to leave no one indifferent—which in itself was no mean feat.

As he grew older, Henry Ford, who for a long period of his life had reigned over an empire, was becoming singularly spoilt. More tyrannical than ever, his fading faculties were a source of real concern to those around him. It was even more worrying as, from 1943, after the death of his son Edsel, the old man had taken over control of a business which was still one of the largest in the world. In 1945 the patriarch was 82 and commonsense told him to stay at home reading his newspapers by the fire-place. In 1945, reading newspapers was interesting for a good American citizen: MacArthur had been in the Pacific since the beginning of the year; President Roosevelt died on 12 April, and from 17 July to 2 August, Churchill, Stalin, and Truman had not been able to finish the Yalta agreements at Potsdam to bring about peace, when the dropping of the atomic bomb on Hiroshima, on 6 August, and on Nagasaki, three days later, called for urgency. However, Clara, Henry's wife, unafraid of causing her terrifying husband a heart-attack, told him plainly that he would be better off giving control to 28-year-old Henry II. At the time this young man was serving dedicatedly in the navy, but he took over Ford on 21 September 1945. He had to make the business move and he did. He set up a team of financial controllers, hitherto unknown at Ford, headed by Colonel Thronton. He also enlisted Robert Mac-Namara's help—he later became the national minister for defence; and Arijoy Miller who was

FORD THUNDERBIRD
CONVERTIBLE
1959

Corvette check mate

later in the service of the US President. To complete this collection of fine people he employed Ernie Breech, one of the best managers at General Motors. This commando was going to shake up the company and launch new projects, of which one was the Thunderbird. For marketing experts it was very clear that the American market was clamouring for a sports car to counter the invasion of foreign makes. Time was pressing as the Corvette project at General Motors already had a year's start. So it was that, at the end of 1954 the Thunderbird made its first appearance. It was virtually an American as seen by Italians. You can imagine it on a background of a strawberry-tiled swimming pool in Hollywood but nowhere else. It had a V8 engine with overhead valves and 4 785 cc but it was soon going to get more pull and more cylinders. In 1956 its spare wheel was put on the outside and in 1958 disaster struck: by giving it more room inside they also made it heavier. It then went and joined the long line of loud, rococo Americans on the discard pile, but doubtless that is what gives it its picturesque charm today.

M
ax Hoffman disembarked in the United
States one fine morning in 1941. In his
hand he had a cheap suitcase and in his
mind an ardent longing to succeed. But "Maxie"
had only one talent when he arrived: he was a born
seller. And that's what he did: he sold cars to
Americans. From the VW to the Jaguar, Hoffman
left his mark on more than one garage. Of course,
Max negotiated with Mercedes too, and in Stuttgart
Hoffman's talents were so talked of, he was
allowed to cover from the East to the West coasts
in a historically unique privilege at Mercedes. Max
was not unhappy but he would have liked the
German company to help the 220 and 300 range to
offer the American market something along the
lines of a Germanic Ferrari: all the more so as the
car existed. That is to say that on 12 March 1952,
Mercedes presented an aggressive 300 SL coupé,
which made its official debut on 5 May of that year
at the famous Mille Miglia. That was fortunate,
because after the Bracco's winning Ferrari saloon,
Kling's Mercedes was second and Caracciola's
fourth.

Then, still in 1952, the American press gasped at
Kling's win in the Carrera Panamericana, a devil-
ishly difficult course battled out in Mexico which
had a considerable following in the United States.
Why not then market a "civilian's" 300 SL? At the
factory they had thought of this but they were
turning a deaf ear; there were other plans and
inevitably other Deutschmarks to invest. They did
not know Maxie well enough. He told no-one that
he was leaving New York one day in July 1953 for
the smog of Stuttgart. There he handed a stupefied
Director a cheque guaranteeing the immediate

MERCEDES-BENZ 300SL
ROADSTER
1961

Max power

purchase of 1 000 300 SL coupés. Of course, the content of this strange meeting has never left the secret archives of Mercedes, but nonetheless at the Salon of New York 1954, Maxie, whose smile was coast to coast wide, presented his 300 SL at an international première. Between 1954 and 1957 1 400 coupés were built and at the Salon of Geneva in 1957 the cabriolet was in the lime-light and 1 858 cars were sold. Its six-cylinder in-line engine developed 215 bhp. When the hood was up it could do 235 kph but required heavy arms and a strong heart because this magnificent feline could sometimes give some unexpected kicks. Ah, for the battles of yesteryear!

The Salon of Geneva is traditionally a place where people of good-breeding get together. Switzerland was not an industrial country, yet, on 15 March, 1961, there was a fine fuss over the Jaguar stand. It was no longer the Salon of Geneva but that of the "E"! William Lyons, the boss of Jaguar, who was phlegmatically smiling, could finally breathe a sigh of relief. He had had a rich 60 years and the E was his last car, the end of his mark on Jaguar's history. It was also a response to the old administration which had asked him to be a little more careful with the money and to be commercially more realistic after five victories for Jaguar at Le Mans between 1951 and 1957.

In 1957, his entourage thought that it was a case of another Trafalgar: this time Jaguar again and again inflicting defeat on its rivals which might prove ruinous if continued. Approving the plan with a malicious smile, William Lyons had to forgo the 24 Hours Race at Le Mans from 1958 to 1959 so as to apply his energy to the E, the plans for which had existed since 1957. Stubborn and ambitious but also very lucid, he nonetheless knew that the time had come to strike hard. After the monumental D, the E had to be better, but this time more appealing to the buyers. It was Malcolm Sawyer, who had already designed the D, who set about researching into the E with a vengeance. His work was brilliant, but what about the other stroke of genius—that of marketing, as it arrived on the

JAGUAR E-TYPE AND E-TYPE S3 V12 ROADSTER
1961 AND 1971

E for all

market at about half the price of its closest rivals: Aston Martin, Porsche, Ferrari and Mercedes. Its engine, from the XK 150S, was a six-cylinder with double overhead camshafts fed by three carburettors. It effortlessly managed 265 bhp and could accelerate from 0 to 60 mph in about 7 seconds. It ended its career in 1975 with a 12-cylinder engine (our red Jaguar). Its success can be understood merely by looking at the number of cabriolets sold. In a little more than 14 years, 33 972 cars were sold.

PORSCHE 356B SUPER 90
CABRIOLET (REUTTER)
1962

The Beetle's baby brother

Ferdinand Porsche, father of the Beetle, had never had the slightest sympathy for Hitler's regime. As with so many other Germans of renown, he had to accept its constraints or, rather, to endure them; but that was enough for blind and vindictive public opinion to keep him away from all that was important to him in his life for a short time after peace had returned. To comfort himself for this humiliation and grief, he did however have the good fortune to have a son, Ferry, who had inherited the family discreetness, and who knew that his father did not wish his Austrian company to remain passive despite his absence. So, with the old paternal guard on the study he worked on a two-seater car which was built in 1947. With a tubular steel chassis covered in aluminium, he had decided that the engine would be central and that he would save as much of the Beetle as he could—practically, the whole of the suspension and transmission. Anyway, his engine had been redesigned and its power rose from 25 bhp to 40 bhp. The aim of this model passed with the building of 500 cars in this range. Unfortunately, with no baggage space at all, with accommodation too limited for two people, this first 356 could not be considered as useful. It was a vehicle of leisure or a second car and nothing else. The second stage was to displace the engine to the rear to make room for two passengers (as long as they were not too voluminous). Similarly, while this time the bodywork was being redesigned they installed a boot. The 356 had been reborn, and lived happily for over 18 years.

165

Of course, it was to undergo numerous modifications throughout its career, like changing the windscreen which was originally in two parts, evoking a curved V-shape. This attention to modernisation was pursued throughout, like arranging the exhausts to exit below the bumpers, while the solid hubcaps were replaced by rims which increased ventilation of the brakes.

In September 1959, the appearance of the 356B was an important stage in this evolution. The front wings were modified, so as to raise the headlights which until then were too low, and the same was done with the bumpers. Finally the rear window arranged in the hood was significantly enlarged to give more acceptable visibility. Throughout its career, the power of the engines was also continuously being developed. The 40 bhp it had in the beginning reached 95 bhp in the 356C.

ALFA ROMEO GIULIA 1600
SPIDER (PININFARINA)
1962

Italian enchantress

Alfa Romeo is Italy, however, the recent history of Alfa Romeo begins in ruins. Those ruins were caused by a terrible bombing raid which destroyed the city of Portello, one balmy October night in 1944. But from 1946 production of automobile and ship engines was restarted, and then, in 1950, the 1900 came out: activity was back to normal. One hundred hours went into building a car as opposed to 240 before the war, a result which was to fill the company directors with optimism. The 1500 cc Alfettas rid themselves of their old styles, and Juan Manuel Fangio and Nino Farina could do the rest. After that it was quite natural for them to think about winning, rather than making profits. Luckily, Giuseppe Luraghi, a clear-minded and stable director, came along and without asking anyone's advice, decided that the company had to produce an average car to fill a gap in the most asked-for sector of the market straightaway. In 1954 the Giulietta, a 1300 cc model, which was to give Alfa Romeo good days until 1962, came out in response to this need. Of course, the Giulia, with 1600 cc, superseded it the following year. This cabriolet, with its body by Pininfarina, sold by virtue of its 172 kph, enough for 9 250 models in this range to be built. This was the car of happy, lazy days. Too much so, perhaps, to survive.

"Your car is a real trap." The expression in the report on the first prototype of the TR series was a little concise but had the advantage of being clear. It came from Ken Richardson, who had only started work a few days before. It came up in a meeting with the boss, Sir John Black. Two hours later, Ken Richardson was given responsibility for trials on the TR project, as Sir John had an idea in mind. He believed that between Jaguar, which was too élitist and too settled, and the MG, which lacked real personality and, above all, youth, there was a place for a small sports car. So, with bits of chassis and pieces of engine, he decided to unveil his first TR, a strange hybrid at the London Salon of 1952. But Black, having wiped some smiles off people's faces, was not going to give up now. There was the TR2, the TR3, then the TR4, which was followed by the TR4A in 1965. It had a more powerful engine and above all an independent rear suspension. A car for which people had a soft spot, as they do for their first girl-friend, even if she lets you down once in a while.

TRIUMPH TR4A IRS
SPORTS CAR
1965

Like the first girl-friend

CHEVROLET CORVETTE STING RAY
CONVERTIBLE
1969

The GM bomber

Driving a Corvette gives the sort of feeling as must be felt by qualified airmen on a touring plane when they take the controls of a Flying Fortress bomber for the first time so that they can go and learn about the technicalities of bombing. At the wheel, he is no longer travelling, but on a mission, and it is war each time his foot is rash enough to push down on the accelerator. However, the car's body is no more flashy than average for large American cars, and as soon as the driver touches the starter, the engine starts with a deceptive purr. It had a V8 engine of 5.7 litres which ensured an instant charge of 233 bhp. It must be remembered that in the 1950s the GM experts began to feel irked by young Americans coming home from Europe and singing the joy of driving Jaguars, Triumphs, MGs and Ferraris. The US market was beginning to get worried, so General Motors began thinking about an American answer. The Waldorf Astoria, no less, in New York, was originally going to be the choice for its presentation one fine day in January 1953. It was difficult to improve on that! The body was in fibreglass and its engine was a six-cylinder of almost four litres, which gave 116 bhp at 3 600 rpm. Its launch was a success: 20 000 order forms completed in the first days, an ecstatic press and a perplexed board of directors.

What were they do do? Make a showy American Corvette or a regular sports car with all the excesses and risks involved with that type of car? The

market soon answered these questions, and its decision was undoubtedly right until the last model of this amazing car was made.

MASERATI GHIBLI
SPYDER (GHIA)
1970

Timeless trident

Winter of 1925 arrived in Bologna without the Maserati brothers taking part in the traditional feasts for more than an hour. They were putting the finishing touches to their first car: the Tipo 26, eight cylinders in line supercharged: 120 bhp and 760 kg. For a while they had only one worry—finding an emblem for their new model. After a little discussion, they decided on the trident that Neptune firmly held above one of the most beautiful fountains in Bologna. It is one of the most well-known achievements of John of Bologna, a Flemish sculptor, in the service of the Duke Francesco de Medici in the 1600s. The Maserati brothers knew his history and wanted to prolong it. So, Mario, the only one of the seven brothers who was not interested in engineering, because he was a painter, gave a less mythical style to the famous trident which will be one of most lasting symbols in the automobile world. Time passed, and in 1966, at the Salon of Turin, the Ghibli was baptised from a design by Ghia. Its V8 4.7 litre engine was derived directly from the Mexico—300 bhp at 5 000 rpm and 280 kph. Two years later, still at the Salon of Turin, this majestically feline cabriolet appeared. It was high time because in the same year, 1968, Adolfo and Omer Orsi, the owners of Maserati, sold most of their shares to Citroën.

179

This car was first unveiled in the Paris Salon of 1968 with a V12 engine of 4.4 litres, four camshafts and six carburettors. It was the most expensive Ferrari ever marketed, and also the fastest. The Spider was presented at the Salon of Frankfurt in 1969, but was sold only from 1971. In both cases the Daytona was one of the most beautiful masterpieces of Pininfarina. This Spider is a rare collectors' piece as 121 examples are in circulation around the world. How Daytona got its name is an interesting subject. In 1966 Ferrari, with a long monopoly on wins at the 24 Hours Race at Le Mans finally had to concede this privilege to Ford. It was at the grey circuit at Daytona Beach in Florida that Ferrari, in its turn, inflicted on Ford an unforgettable humiliation. The public's imagination saw in the 365 GT a desire to settle scores dating back to Daytona and to give it the name of the field of this historic battle. Mr Ferrari, who had already foreseen this possibility, had his own ideas and refused to name the car after public opinion, which is why Daytona is only a nickname.

FERRARI 365 GTS/4
SPIDER (SCAGLIETTI)
1972

The Diva

CITROËN SM
MYLORD (CHAPRON)
1972

The odd couple

In 1968, against all expectations, Citroën bought up Maserati. Why? Twenty years later the last page of the novel of suppositions has still not been written, but one thing is certain: Citroën, which had long been dreaming about a prestige car, was finally going to find the sort of engine and engineering which for a long time had been absent from the atmosphere of the Quai de Javel. Alfieri, the Magician at Maserati, cut two cylinders off the V8 of the Maserati Indy so as not to pass the fearful tax limits above 16 horsepower and his work was done. In Paris, Opron and Giret took responsibility for its looks and aerodynamics. Eighteen months later, the SM became the sensation at the Salon of Geneva in 1970. Some people were sceptical (quite normal for Citroën), but car enthusiasts were intrigued and shocked and, when all is said and done, the car was another great success. Then, certain developments needed to be made but the car was so basically sound that at the end of its career 12 856 almost identical SMs had been sold.

More than one bodybuilder was overwhelmed with the desire for a cabriolet. The roof of the SM had in fact been reinforced to help to hold the lower part rigid; getting rid of it would be tempting trouble. The only people to try were Heuliez with "Espace", with a gimmick which did not comply with the definition for a cabriolet, and Chapron, who was much more orthodox. This cabriolet by Chapron appeared in the Salon of Paris in 1971 and only eight models were sold.

ROLLS-ROYCE CORNICHE
CONVERTIBLE (MULLINER–PARK WARD)
1981

The silent phoenix

In 1970 Rolls-Royce suffered a fate worse than death. In the hallowed place of prestige and history came the authoritarian and merciless administration of the Official Receiver. Lawrence of Arabia and Rudyard Kipling, both former clients for the make, turned in their graves: the adventure and legend of Rolls had just come to join them.

After talk of bad product selection, bad management, outdated commercial politics, came the news: Rolls-Royce had not a single penny to its name. Soon the British sense of honour made the Rolls affair a great national cause.

At Rolls, it is widely believed, as far as men and engines are concerned no changes are ever made, only modifications. Thus, another director appeared quietly at the helm of the new company, David Plastow, who had been thinking of this for a long time as his father was already Sales Director of the famous make. But Plastow, who soon began to study the market, did so with the eye of a generation which was more flexible in outlook. The Corniche, which is something of a prototype finished by a new generation, was born out of this frame of mind.

Presented in 1971, the Corniche was the first Rolls in the Shadow series to house a V8, 6 750 cc engine. The body's design belongs to H J Mulliner-Park Ward, a sort of consortium.

ASTON MARTIN V8
VOLANTE
1984

Traditional masterpiece

This model, which was aimed primarily at the American market, was practically sheltered from any competition because its price reached such dizzy heights that only piles of dollars could reach it. Its success, since its production is superior to that of the coupé, lies in its shape: a sort of majesty installed in an abnegation of the ostentatious. The dignity is a classic of English parade. This car weighs 1 780 kg and its body received ten careful layers of paint because such a robe could not bear even the slightest speck of dust. The great V8 with 5 340 cc could achieve almost 400 bhp (the builder wouldn't reveal its power). From the first to the last part each car is assembled by a single man, in the untarnished tradition of the goldsmiths of the king of the Middle Ages. Once this masterpiece was completed it was signed by its author on a plate stuck to one of the camshaft covers.

This car is 20 years old. Daily demand has never gone below 45—allowing the builder to earn twice as much money as even the most optimistic calculations could have envisaged. However, when the 928 was born, in all its arrogance and modernness, the days of the 911 seemed numbered. The 944 was less of a Porsche, but more approachable. The 911 engine was still at the rear and success kept following it. It went further and further. From 1978, the 911 was complacent, and made no progress in its specifications. It was as if Porsche had said of its clients: "If they like it we'll leave it at that". The figures it managed—and there was no competition even close—are fascinating: 231 bhp in an engine of 3 164 cc, 245 kph maximum speed, 0–60 mph in about 6 seconds, 0–100 mph in 15.1 seconds. After that what else can be said, apart from enthusing about the treasures of a wondrous technology. The ignition's advance curve is memorised by a computer. The gearbox is equipped with a small oil-cooler whose circulation pump is housed in the casing of the differential. The Carrera is the future now and the future of tradition.

PORSCHE 911 CARRERA
CABRIOLET
1984

A twenty-year vintage

At the beginning of March in Geneva, while great flakes stormed across the grey arches of the Mont Blanc bridge, the Automobile salon was opening its doors. The Mondial was enthroned on the Ferrari stand but some fanatics of the make were obviously feeling extremely uncomfortable, others were sulking, but it was still sadness which united the majority. Mr Ferrari was not there, but the echo of this mediocre success reached him. The lines, signed by Pininfarina, had not been well accepted by everyone. It was too functional, over-futuristic: the Mondial was impressive but lacked class. Even worse, the V8 engine had only 16 valves, and had to admit that to carry about 1 430 kg, its 214 bhp was too low a figure. It had to gather up speed to reach 220 kph with the risk, insulting for the Ferrari lover, of being overtaken by a lesser, nay, even a cheaper, car. From the 1983 models onwards, Mr Ferrari accepted he had made a mistake and adopted 32 valves. With 240 bhp the Quattrovalvole was finally accepted into the ranks of the Ferrari, and its recorded speed of 240 kph restored to the driver a holy man's belief that he has found his faith again.

FERRARI MONDIAL QUATTROVALVOLE
CABRIOLET (PININFARINA)
1985

Modena magic

TECHNICAL DATA

Manufacturer	**Ballot**
Model	2 LT
Body type	3-seater Torpedo
Coachbuilder	Lagache, Glaszmann & Co.
Engine type	4 cylinders in line (single o.h.c.)
Cylinder capacity	1995 cc (69.9 × 130 mm)
Maximum power	—
Wheelbase	2.794 m
Years built	1923–1928
Number built	Approximately 2 000

Manufacturer	**Rolls-Royce**
Model	Springfield Phantom I
Body type	Piccadilly Roadster
Coachbuilder	Brewster
Engine type	6 cylinders in line
Cylinder capacity	7668 cc (107.93 × 139.7)
Maximum power	100 bhp at 2 750 rpm
Wheelbase	3.645 m
Years built	1926–1931
Number built	1 225 (including all types of body)

Manufacturer	**Delage**
Model	D8 SS
Body type	Cabriolet
Coachbuilder	Fernandez & Darrin
Engine type	8 cylinders in line
Cylinder capacity	4060 cc (77 × 109 mm)
Maximum power	118 bhp at 3 800 rpm
Wheelbase	3.31 m
Years built	1929–1933
Number built	99 (D8S and SS combined)

Manufacturer	**Rolls-Royce**
Model	Phantom II
Body type	Convertible
Coachbuilder	Fountain's
Engine type	6L
Cylinder capacity	7668 cc (107.93 × 139.7 mm)
Maximum power	Not revealed
Wheelbase	3.66 m
Years built	1929–1935
Number built	1 767

Manufacturer	**Packard**
Model	Twelve Series II
Body type	Cabriolet
Coachbuilder	—
Engine type	V12 at 67 degrees
Cylinder capacity	7292 cc (87.3 × 101.6 mm)
Maximum power	160 bhp at 3 200 rpm
Wheelbase	3.60 m
Years built	1934
Number built	960 examples in 1934 (out of 5 298 "Twelves")

Manufacturer	**Panhard**
Model	6 CS type X-72
Body type	2- to 5-seater Belen Cabriolet
Coachbuilder	Panhard
Engine type	6 cylinders in line (valveless)
Cylinder capacity	2 516 cc (72 × 103 mm)
Maximum power	65 bhp at 3 500 rpm
Wheelbase	3.17 m
Years built	1932–1934
Number built	—

Manufacturer	**Mercedes-Benz**
Model	500 K
Body type	Cabriolet B
Coachbuilder	Sindelfingen
Engine type	8 cylinders in line, supercharged
Cylinder capacity	5019 cc (86 × 108 mm)
Maximum power	160 bhp at 3400 rpm
Wheelbase	3.29 m
Years built	1934–1936
Number built	354 (all body types combined)

Manufacturer	**Delahaye**
Model	135 competition
Body type	Cabriolet
Coachbuilder	Chapron
Engine type	6 cylinders in line
Cylinder capacity	3558 cc (84 × 107 mm)
Maximum power	120 bhp at 4200 rpm
Wheelbase	2.95 m
Years built	1935–1938
Number built	—

Manufacturer	**Rolls-Royce**
Model	Twenty
Body type	Drophead Coupé
Coachbuilder	Southern Motor Co (1936)
Engine type	6 cylinders in line
Cylinder capacity	3127 cc (76.2 × 114.3 mm)
Maximum power	Not revealed
Wheelbase	3.276 mm
Years built	1922–1929
Number built	1 (out of 2 940 "Twenty"s)

Manufacturer	**Ford**
Model	V8–78
Body type	Club Cabriolet
Coachbuilder	—
Engine type	V8 at 90 degrees
Cylinder capacity	3624 cc (78 × 95 mm)
Maximum power	85 bhp at 3800 rpm
Wheelbase	2.845 m
Years built	1937
Number built	7 618 "Club Cabriolet" 37, out of 1 008 793

Manufacturer	**Peugeot**
Model	402
Body type	Electric convertible (type E4)
Coachbuilder	—
Engine type	4 cylinders in line
Cylinder capacity	1991 cc (83 × 93 mm)
Maximum power	55 bhp
Wheelbase	3.15 m
Years built	1935–1937
Number built	39 500 (all body types combined, short wheelbase)

Manufacturer	**Hispano-Suiza**
Model	K6
Body type	—
Coachbuilder	Kellner
Engine type	6 cylinders in line
Cylinder capacity	5184 cc (100 × 110 mm)
Maximum power	140 bhp at 3500 rpm
Wheelbase	3.42/3.72 m
Years built	1934–1937
Number built	204 (all body types combined)

Manufacturer	**Horch**
Model	853 A
Body type	Sport Cabriolet
Coachbuilder	—
Engine type	8 cylinders in line (single o.h.c.)
Cylinder capacity	4994 cc (87 × 104 mm)
Maximum power	120 bhp at 3400 rpm
Wheelbase	3.45 m
Years built	1938–1939
Number built	1 023 (853 and 853 A, all models combined)

Manufacturer	**Citroën**
Model	11B
Body type	3- to 5-seater Cabriolet
Coachbuilder	—
Engine type	4 cylinders in line
Cylinder capacity	1911 cc (78 × 100 mm)
Maximum power	46 bhp at 3800 rpm
Wheelbase	3.09 m
Years built	1934–1939
Number built	510 (in 1938 and 1939)

Manufacturer	**Bugatti**
Model	57 SC
Body type	Drophead Coupé
Coachbuilder	Corsica
Engine type	8 cylinders in line (double o.h.c.)
Cylinder capacity	3257 cc (57 × 100 mm)
Maximum power	210 bhp
Wheelbase	2.98 m
Years built	1936–1938
Number built	Approximately 40 (S and SC, all body types combined)

Manufacturer	**Talbot (Darracq)**
Model	Lago T-150SS
Body type	Cabriolet
Coachbuilder	Figoni & Falaschi
Engine type	6 cylinders in line (hemispherical cylinder head)
Cylinder capacity	3996 cc (90 × 104 mm)
Maximum power	140 bhp at 4100 rpm
Wheelbase	2.65 m
Years built	1937–1939
Number built	—

Manufacturer	**Lagonda**
Model	LG 6
Body type	Drophead Coupé
Coachbuilder	—
Engine type	6 cylinders in line
Cylinder capacity	4453 cc (88.5 × 120.6 mm)
Maximum power	150 bhp
Wheelbase	3.226/3.429 m
Years built	1938–1940
Number built	82 (all body types combined)

Manufacturer	**Delahaye**
Model	165
Body type	Cabriolet
Coachbuilder	Figoni & Falaschi
Engine type	V12
Cylinder capacity	4496 cc (75 × 84.7 mm)
Maximum power	170 bhp at 4500 rpm
Wheelbase	3.21 m
Years built	1938
Number built	Approximately 5

Manufacturer	**Lincoln**
Model	Zephyr
Body type	760-B Convertible Coupé
Coachbuilder	—
Engine type	V12 at 75 degrees
Cylinder capacity	4380 cc (69.8 × 95.2 mm)
Maximum power	110 bhp at 3900 rpm
Wheelbase	3.175 m
Years built	1938
Number built	600

Manufacturer	**Alfa Romeo**
Model	6 c 2500 S
Body type	4-seater Cabriolet
Coachbuilder	Touring
Engine type	6 cylinders in line
Cylinder capacity	2443 cc (72 × 100 mm)
Maximum power	95 bhp at 4600 rpm
Wheelbase	3.00 m
Years built	1939–1952
Number built	779 (all body types combined)

Manufacturer	**Chrysler**
Model	C-39
Body type	Town and Country
Coachbuilder	—
Engine type	8 cylinders in line
Cylinder capacity	5305 cc (84.1 × 112.6 mm)
Maximum power	135 bhp at 3400 rpm
Wheelbase	3.238 m
Years built	1946–1948
Number built	8 380 (of which 135 were built in 1946)

Manufactuer	**Bentley**
Model	Mark VI
Body type	Drophead Foursome Coupé
Coachbuilder	Park Ward
Engine type	6 cylinders in line
Cylinder capacity	4527 cc (88.9 × 114.3 mm)
Maximum power	Not revealed
Wheelbase	3.048 m
Years built	1946–1952
Number built	4 000 with 4.25 litre engine (of which 128 has Park Ward coachwork)

Manufacturer	**Jaguar**
Model	Mark V
Body type	Drophead Coupé
Coachbuilder	—
Engine type	6 cylinders in line
Cylinder capacity	3485 cc (82 × 110 mm)
Maximum power	125 bhp at 4500 rpm
Wheelbase	2.54 m
Years built	—
Number built	972 (plus 29 d.h.c. with 2.5 litre engine)

Manufacturer	**Studebaker**
Model	Champion
Body type	Regal Convertible
Coachbuilder	—

Engine type	6 cylinders in line
Cylinder capacity	2779 cc (100.3 × 101.6 mm)
Maximum power	85 bhp
Wheelbase	2.921
Years built	1950–1951
Number built	8 027 (of the 1951 Convertible)

Manufacturer	**Aston Martin**
Model	DB 2
Body type	Drophead Coupé
Coachbuilder	—
Engine type	6 cylinders in line (double o.h.c.)
Cylinder capacity	2580 cc (78 × 90 mm)
Maximum power	105 bhp at 5 000 rpm
Wheelbase	2.525 m
Years built	1950–1953
Number built	401 (including the Fixed Head Coupé)

Manufacturer	**Lincoln**
Model	Capri Special Custom
Body type	Convertible
Coachbuilder	—
Engine type	V8 at 90 degrees
Cylinder capacity	5 201 cc (96.5 × 88.9 mm)
Maximum power	205 bhp at 4 200 rpm
Wheelbase	3.125 m
Years built	1954
Number built	1951

Manufacturer	**Facel-Véga**
Model	FVS/FV1
Body type	Cabriolet
Coachbuilder	Chrysler
Engine type	V8 at 90 degrees
Cylinder capacity	4 770 cc (94.5 × 84.9)
Maximum power	200 bhp at 4 400 rpm

Wheelbase	2.63 m
Years built	1955
Number built	Approximately 5 (out of about 20 FV/FV1)

Manufactuer	**BMW**
Model	507
Body type	Touring Sport Roadster
Coachbuilder	BMW
Engine type	V8 at 90 degrees
Cylinder capacity	3 168 cc (82 × 75 mm)
Maximum power	150 bhp at 5 000 rpm
Wheelbase	2.48 m
Years built	1955–1959
Number built	252

Manufacturer	**Lancia**
Model	Aurelia/GT 2500
Body type	Convertible B 24S
Coachbuilder	Pininfarina
Engine type	V6 at 60 degrees
Cylinder capacity	2 451 cc (78 × 85.5 mm)
Maximum power	118 bhp at 5 300 rpm
Wheelbase	2.45 m
Years built	1956–1959
Number built	520 (plus 240 Spider America)

Manufacturer	**Cadillac**
Model	Sixty-Two
Body type	Convertible Coupé (type 6267)
Coachbuilder	—
Engine type	V8 at 90 degrees
Cylinder capacity	6 390 cc (101.6 × 98.4 mm)
Maximum power	325 bhp at 4 800 rpm
Wheelbase	3.302 m
Years built	1959
Number built	11 130 (in the year of the '59 model)

Manufacturer	**Jaguar**
Model	XK 150
Body type	Drophead Coupé
Coachbuilder	—
Engine type	6 cylinders in line (double o.h.c.)
Cylinder capacity	3 442 cc
Maximum power	213 bhp at 5 500 rpm
Wheelbase	2.59 m
Years built	1957–1960
Number built	2 671 (of a total of 9 398 XK 150s)

Manufacturer	**Ford**
Model	Thunderbird
Body type	Convertible (76-A)
Coachbuilder	—
Engine type	V8 at 90 degrees
Cylinder capacity	7 046 cc (109.2 × 93.38 mm)
Maximum power	350 bhp at 4 400 rpm
Wheelbase	2.87 m
Years built	1959
Number built	10 261 (of a total of 67 456 T-bird, 1959)

Manufacturer	**Mercedes-Benz**
Model	300 SL (W-198 II)
Body type	Roadster
Coachbuilder	—
Engine type	6 cylinders in line (single o.h.c., fuel injection)
Cylinder capacity	2 996 cc (85 × 88 mm)
Maximum power	225 bhp at 5 900 rpm
Wheelbase	2.40 m
Years built	1957–1963
Number built	1 858 (of a total of 3 258 "300 SL"s)

Manufacturer	**Jaguar**
Model	E-Type
Body type	Open Two-Seater

Coachbuilder	—
Engine type	6 cylinders in line (double o.h.c.)
Cylinder capacity	3 781 cc (87 × 106 mm)
Maximum power	269 bhp at 5 500 rpm
Wheelbase	2.44 m
Years built	1961–1964
Number built	7 820 (of a total of 15 490 "E-Type 3.8 litres")

Manufacturer	**Jaguar**
Model	E-Type S3 V12
Body type	Roadster
Coachbuilder	—
Engine type	V12 at 60 degrees (2 × single o.h.c.)
Cylinder capacity	5 343 cc (90 × 70 mm)
Maximum power	268 bhp at 5 750 rpm
Wheelbase	2.67 m
Years built	1971–1975
Number built	7 990 (of a total of 15 290 "E-Type S3"s)

Manufacturer	**Porsche**
Model	356B Super 90
Body type	Cabriolet
Coachbuilder	Reutter
Engine type	6 cylinders flat
Cylinder capacity	1 528 cc (82.5 × 74 mm)
Maximum power	90 bhp at 5 500 rpm
Wheelbase	2.10 m
Years built	1960–1963
Number built	30 963 (all 356B models combined)

Manufacturer	**Alfa Romeo**
Model	Giulia 1600
Body type	Spider
Coachbuilder	Pininfarina
Engine type	4 cylinders in line (double o.h.c.)

Cylinder capacity	1 570 cc (78 × 82 mm)
Maximum power	92 bhp at 6 200 rpm
Wheelbase	2.25 m
Years built	1962–1965
Number built	9 250 (plus 1 091 "Veloce" 112 bhp)

Manufacturer	**Triumph**
Model	TR4A IRS
Body type	Sports car
Coachbuilder	—
Engine type	4 cylinders in line
Cylinder capacity	2 138 cc (86 × 92 mm)
Maximum power	100 bhp at 4 600 rpm
Wheelbase	2.24 m
Years built	1965–1967
Number built	28 465 (of a total of 68 714 "TR4"s)

Manufacturer	**Chevrolet**
Model	Corvette Sting Ray
Body type	Convertible
Coachbuilder	—
Engine type	V8 at 90 degrees
Cylinder capacity	6 996 cc (107.98 × 95.5 mm)
Maximum power	390 bhp at 5 400 rpm
Wheelbase	2.49 m
Years built	1969
Number built	16 608 (of 38 762 examples of the 1969 model)

Manufacturer	**Maserati**
Model	Ghibli
Body type	Spyder
Coachbuilder	Ghia
Engine type	V8 at 90 degrees (2 × double o.h.c.)
Cylinder capacity	4 719 cc
Maxmum power	330 bhp at 5 000 rpm

Wheelbase	2.55 m
Years built	1969–1972
Number built	125 (of a total of 1 274 Ghibli)

Manufacturer	**Ferrari**
Model	365 GTS/4
Body type	Spider
Coachbuilder	Scaglietti
Engine type	V12 (2 × double o.h.c.)
Cylinder capacity	4 390 cc (81 × 71 mm)
Maximum power	352 bhp at 7 500 rpm
Wheelbase	2.40 m
Years built	1969–1973
Number built	127

Manufacturer	**Citroën**
Model	SM
Body type	"Mylord"
Coachbuilder	Chapron
Engine type	V6 at 60 degrees (2 × double o.h.c.)
Cylinder capacity	2 670 cc (87 × 75 mm)
Maximum power	170 bhp at 5 500 rpm
Wheelbase	2.95 m

Years built	1971–1974
Number built	8 (of a total of 12 290 "SM"s)

Manufacturer	**Rolls-Royce**
Model	Corniche
Body type	Convertible
Coachbuilder	Mulliner-Park Ward
Engine type	V8 at 90 degrees
Cylinder capacity	6 750 cc (104.1 × 99.1 mm)
Maximum power	Not revealed
Wheelbase	3.05 m
Years built	1971
Number built	—

Manufacturer	**Aston Martin**
Model	V8
Body type	Volante
Coachbuilder	—
Engine type	V8 at 90 degrees (2 × double o.h.c.)
Cylinder capacity	5 340 cc (100 × 85 mm)
Maximum power	Not revealed
Wheelbase	2.61 m
Years built	1978

Number built	—

Manufacturer	**Porsche**
Model	911 Carrera
Body type	Cabriolet
Coachbuilder	—
Engine type	6 cylinders flat (2 × single o.h.c.)
Cylinder capacity	3 164 cc
Maximum power	231 bhp at 5 900 rpm
Wheelbase	2.27 m
Years built	1983
Number built	—

Manufacturer	**Ferrari**
Model	Mondial Quattrovalvole
Body type	Cabriolet
Coachbuilder	Pininfarina
Engine type	V8 (4 o.h.c., 32 valves)
Cylinder capacity	2 927 cc
Maximum power	240 bhp at 7 000 rpm
Wheelbase	2.65 m
Years built	1984
Number built	—

Achevé d'imprimer
sur les presses de l'imprimerie Berger-Levrault
en mai 1986 ·